WE WILL NOT DIE HERE

with love,

Zack Redman

ZACK REDMAN

 FriesenPress

Suite 300 - 990 Fort St
Victoria, BC, V8V 3K2
Canada

www.friesenpress.com

ISBN
978-1-03-911656-6 (Hardcover)
978-1-03-911655-9 (Paperback)
978-1-03-911657-3 (eBook)

1. HISTORY, MILITARY, WORLD WAR II

Distributed to the trade by The Ingram Book Company

WE WILL NOT DIE HERE

Author's Note

First and foremost, I would like to thank you, the reader, for deciding that this book is worth your time to read. Whether you have purchased it yourself or it has been given to you as a gift, the fact that you now hold it in your hands honours me deeply.

I never intended to be a writer. Calling myself an *author* feels strange. It is even stranger to see my name at the top of a book cover. But I have always had a love for storytelling.

As a young man, and up to this day, I have considered myself a musician. I told stories through that medium and it remains a great passion of mine. But I have continuously found it harder and harder to tell the stories I *need* to share in a format that only allots three to five minutes of time. Thus, the leap from songwriting to storytelling was made.

I have always had a fascination with war. The bravery and the sacrifice. And I still believe there is no work of fiction created meant to shock and terrify that can surpass the real horrors of those periods in our history.

I read many memoirs from the men who survived World War II, both American and German, as well as those who survived the Holocaust, in preparation for this book. I watched countless interviews of men brought to tears as they told their stories of that time, and have tried to represent their spirits and struggles as truthfully as I could, no matter how dark and unimaginable the things they had to do were.

Within these pages there will of course be things that I got wrong as well as creative liberties I used to accomplish my narrative. But many of the things you are about to read are true. Things that were witnessed, things that some took part in, and things that I won't ever be able to forget.

I wanted to be accurate to the events of that time when telling this story. Though Henry Gerald Briggs and Dieter Von Strauss never existed, what they both experienced surely did, and they became my conduit to share the cruel realities of war with you.

When finished with this book, and you want to hear more about this unfathomable time in human history, I implore you to read the memoirs of the firsthand accounts of men who were there and fought in World War II. The courage these men had to throw themselves into the hell of war cannot be understated or—more importantly—forgotten. The world would truly be a different place without their strength and unwavering resolve in the face of certain peril.

To say that I've dedicated this book to them seems like a miniscule display of my appreciation for everything they did, but I do so with the utmost sincerity for my gratitude to what they endured and accomplished, and my admiration for them as men.

-Zack Redman

P.S. Thanks, Chris, for lending me HBO's *Band Of Brothers*, which began this entire journey.

PART I:

IN THE PINES

"It is foolish and wrong to mourn the men who died.
Rather, we should thank God that such men lived."
-George S. Patton Jr.

One

I am a coward and a fool, but one thing I am not, is ashamed.

Have you ever seen a motion picture you just couldn't finish? It was reviewed highly in the papers and won all sorts of awards, but once you sat down to watch it, it just didn't connect. You try and try but the story is going nowhere. You say: *I'll give it five more minutes,* and maybe a scene or two pulls your attention in for a brief moment, then it's back to how it was before. War is kind of like that. At what point do you just turn it off and walk away?

My name is Private Henry Gerald Briggs. I served in Easy Company, 2nd Battalion of the 506th Parachute Infantry Regiment of the 101st Airborne Division as a replacement, and I am a deserter.

On December 16, 1944, in a last-ditch effort to push back Allied forces from entering Germany, Hitler sent everything he had left at us in the Ardennes Woods of

Belgium. We were huddled in fox holes near the German-occupied village of Foy to avoid the constant shelling.

The snowy conditions often brought the temperature to as low as -20 Fahrenheit by night. To make things worse, we were wholly under-supplied. We were given neither appropriate clothing for such temperatures nor sufficient amounts of ammunition to advance an attack, so in those frozen fox holes, we simply held our ground.

The skies above were heavily clouded over, making supply drops impossible with any amount of accuracy. Fires were forbidden as the smoke could reveal our positions to the enemy. K-rations were scarce and all but gone. Medical supplies were dwindling fast as men were wounded, and the constant barrage of small arms fire and mortar fire meant you were never at ease. Those few weeks were the worst of my life.

The men of Easy Company were some of the bravest and most resilient men I had ever met. They would get wounded in combat and sneak out from the hospitals to rejoin their comrades in battle. They were all fearless. They were heroes. I was not.

After weeks of battling mortars, gunfire, freezing temperatures, frostbite, trench-foot, and hunger, I simply walked away in the night. I could not handle it in the way the other men of Easy could. I lasted eleven days in that fox hole, where I sheltered, shivered, and shat. I simply could not do it any longer.

I can't recall the exact day that I left the cratered and battered frontline in the Bois Jacques woods, south of Foy, with its treetops blown to splinters and the limbs of both

4

the densely packed pines and my comrades scattered in the snow. I had no destination in mind, I just had to get away. We were surrounded on all sides but the weather conditions were so bad, I managed to make it out of the combat zone undetected. Those woods outside of Foy were ghostly. There was a dense fog that choked all visibility and the snow made it a haunting scene amongst all that death.

Seeing snow on the battlefield changed the entire landscape, not just visibly, but it changed how it felt to be at war. We were used to dirt and mud and rain, but this was ethereal. The way blood stands out in the virgin snow is a sight that perverts the mind.

After two days of walking, the whistling of shells, clatter of gunfire, and the screams of wounded men still crept through the trees. I passed bodies as I walked, of both men and horses, disfigured and crooked with death, frozen stiff, some with twisted arms outstretched, some looking peaceful in their eternal rest in the snow. If their flesh hadn't been chewed up by heavy artillery or grenades then it had been done so by animals. You could always tell if it had been a rat or some other kind of rodent due to the wounds appearing sickly white or a pale pink. Blood that had long frozen in the body never reached those wounds.

The woods seemed to go on forever, especially with the snow dampening my pace. When your eyes weren't solely focused on the flashing barrels of enemy infantry, you could stop to observe your surroundings in peace. The sun, which filtered down through clouds and fog like water in a colander, softened the light and gave everything a bright angelic glow. The addition of a heavy blanket of white snow made everything seem heaven-like, and for brief moments throughout the following days, I thought maybe I had indeed died and this was heaven after all, but the cold and hunger would quickly reassure my ties to this mortal plain.

On the third day I watched as a horse came limping out from the fog. One of its front legs had been blown to splinters as it continued its morose lumbering and I pulled my pistol and put it out of its misery. Seeing men eviscerated and dying was one thing, but seeing such an elegant and beautiful animal suffer hurt the heart in different and depressing ways. I fed on that horse with pain in my soul through the night.

At first light I continued on through the trees. I spent the night huddled under the horse. It offered warmth for a while before the body went cold. I had heard of men opening up the bellies of animals such as this and crawling inside, though I could not bring myself to do it. I figured the blood would soon freeze and I would be in a worse state than I already was.

I was still afraid to start a fire. Everything was damp and nothing creates more smoke than wet wood. The fog was still heavy and omnipresent; I almost convinced myself even then that the smoke from my fire would not be seen, but I didn't want to risk it. Now I had two armies to try and stay hidden from: the Germans, who would almost certainly prolong my death in the most unspeakable ways, and the Americans, who would either shoot me on the spot for desertion or drag me back home to try me for my crime. At times that seemed like a reasonable punishment. It may mean I *would* be returning home, though I would live the rest of my life labelled a traitor. Though at times, in this unbearable cold, a warm jail cell seemed like a welcome reprieve.

I had grown up on a farm just outside of New Hope, Pennsylvania. My father had purchased the land after returning home from The Great War. I was born August 4, 1919, and was the oldest of four, the only boy. I never wanted to join the army after hearing the horrors of my father's experience, but when my sisters were old enough to take over my responsibilities on the farm, and a month after my twenty-fifth birthday, my father drove me into town to enlist. I was then shuttled to Camp Toccoa in Georgia to complete my four months of training. I would have been fine with a desk job filing papers, a welcome break from the hard labor of farm life. But my father was adamant I become a paratrooper. It was new and one of the most dangerous jobs during the war, but it paid an extra $50 on top of your standard $50 wage, and my father said the farm would benefit greatly from that money.

Training was hard, even for me, a farm boy. We ran all day and we ran all night. We crawled through mud, sparred with bayonet rifles, jumped from fake planes onto flat grasslands, then ran some more.

When I was fourteen, I was pulled from school to work for my dad. I always detested him for that. I never learned the proper social skills one obtains from a school environment, especially through those teenage years when everything is peculiar and changing. Because of

7

this I didn't form that unusual bond men acquire in training, that bond you hear of from men who survived combat. But there was one man I was very fond of: Eugene Leopold Blyth.

Eugene was a pencil-thin city boy from Cleveland, Ohio. He told people he was eighteen, though he was hardly seventeen when he enlisted. His arms were ropey and he had a lush head of orangish-golden hair before we got our cuts, but not even a hint of hair on his face. I immediately liked him. His timidity was relatable and we connected on that level. Eugene became the brother I never had during those four months of training. I loved that man like family. He died the first day of combat.

When we arrived in Belgium, most of the men I trained with were dispersed. Luckily, Eugene and I were kept together and were swiftly assigned to the 101st.

The Battle of the Ardennes was my first introduction to combat, and it was, in every sense of the phrase, trial by fire.

Eugene and I shared a fox hole. We dug ferociously that first day in the Ardennes Woods and had made respectable progress. My hands were already hardened with calluses from years of farm work but Eugene struggled with the digging. Though I knew it was hard for him, and his hands bled, he never complained. He was a tough son of a bitch.

The earth was frozen and dense with tree roots. That on top of the periodical shelling and bursts of gunfire made an already difficult job an excruciating endeavor, but by nightfall we had it done.

It was then that our first, and subsequently only, supply of K-rations was handed out. Eugene and I spoke like brothers do. We slung insults and jabbed each other with soft fists. I told him that I had finished my side of the fox hole first; therefore, it was his job to retrieve the K-rations. Eugene, having two brothers of his own, knew all the tender spots to hit you. He slugged me in the lower thigh just above the kneecap and my leg shot with pain. I booted him in the rear end as he crawled from our fox hole and he lost his footing and fell forward. I hadn't heard the shot until his helmet tumbled from his head. An onslaught of gunfire proceeded and, instinctively, I cowered to the bottom of the pit that I had spent most of the day digging. All my training was thrown into the wind as I dropped my rifle and threw my hands over my helmet. A fellow comrade who had been caught in the exchange ran over to my hole, grabbing Eugene by the front of his shirt, and dragging his lifeless body in with him. This man, by the name of "Wild Bill" Guarnere, grabbed my rifle from the dirt of my shallow fox hole and thrust it into my chest.

"Point it that way and shoot, soldier!" He commanded in his thick Philly accent, and I did so, only managing a brief glance at my fallen friend, whose eyes looked back at me empty, holding no light.

In war, it is said that if you can hear the shot then it wasn't meant for you. There was no way Eugene heard that shot.

Through teary eyes I raised my rifle and began to fire. Though the only things I most likely managed to hit were trees in front of me and the dirt surrounding them, I did so with fervor.

The following ten days were like this. Huddle for warmth in your fox holes, cower from shellings, then return fire. I was spent in every sense of the word. My stomach ached with hunger, my body shook from the cold, my nerves ran throughout my skin like live wires from the constant tension of the next assured fire-fight, and my mind frayed like cheap cloth. It was then, on the eleventh day of this, that I walked off into the night.

Two

With a belly still full of raw horse heart, liver, and kidney, I pressed on through the woods. When coming across open fields, I would submerge myself back into the trees. All the surrounding towns were thick with fighting, fighting of which I steered clear.

My feet were immensely cold. I was afraid to check them for what I might see—skin blackened from frost-bite—followed by an impending anxiety that I might not be able to carry on.

On my sixth day of walking I came across a farm house in a barren field that undoubtedly once harbored barley, corn, or wheat. It reminded me of home, a thought I despairingly ushered from my mind despite its relative comfort. I was afraid to leave the protection of the woods; their concealment had gotten me this far unharmed. By the way things went, I would take a single step out into the open and be shot dead instantly. But something drew me to that farm house. Perhaps a cow rested within the barn that sat off to the right of the house, maybe even chickens. Was the uncertain promise of milk and eggs worth the risk of leaving the refuge of these all-too-familiar trees? I crossed that featureless field adorned with snow and I didn't look back.

I felt a childish fear come over me as I sprinted toward the farm house. It was a feeling I had as a boy when swimming in the Aquetong Lake back home in Pennsylvania. I would dive from the docks into the chilly water and be struck with the thought of a lake monster at my heels. I knew such things to be nothing more than fantasy, but still I would hurry back to the dock in a subdued panic. Here, that primordial colossus was very much real. It was the towering colossus of war.

Safely across, I went to the barn first with my rifle drawn. Whether I would have fired upon whatever or whomever I may have found in there, I was not sure, but I held that rifle firm all the same.

To my dismay, the barn was empty. There was no semblance of life at all. I then turned my attention to the farm house.

How I gathered the courage to bark out my presence, I do not know, but no one returned my call. The front door was unlocked and I pushed it open with the barrel of my gun.

The door swung open, braying its reluctance with creaks and moans, and I entered the home. The place was abandoned, or so I thought.

I was greeted by an immediate hallway with a footworn flight of stairs leading to the second floor. To my left, a dining room, to my right, a living room with a brick fireplace against the far wall. The place had been ransacked. Pictures hung on the walls, crooked and dry muddy footprints littered the hardwood floors.

It was common for US soldiers to loot as they cleared their way across Belgium—or so I had been told. Everyone wanted souvenirs to take home with them once the war had ended. For some, it was nothing more than an indulgence of a newly found power these men had never experienced before. For others, the looting ignited a frenzy within. For most, taking souvenirs reassured a feeling that they might make it home after all to enjoy them.

Drawers laid lazily on the floors, having been emptied of their contents. Women's clothing was scattered throughout the rooms. All the blankets had been taken.

I cleared the first floor without resistance, my heart pounding against my ribcage like a mallet. When I crept up the U-shaped staircase with my rifle still raised, I was met at gunpoint by a German soldier, his Luger fixed on my head.

"Stop, or I'll shoot!" he barked.

English? I thought. *That was a surprise.*

"Lower your weapon!" I barked back, and we continued to shout commands over one another.

I am a coward, as I stated earlier, but in a moment like this, with your heart racing and your knuckles white around your weapon, a primal instinct for survival takes over.

I was prepared to shoot if need be, but before I had a chance, the German fired his weapon. The bullet went high and zinged over my head. The German went to fire again but the bullet became jammed in the pistol's action. He looked at it confused for the useless piece of machinery it was, then hurled it at me. The Luger glanced off the barrel of my rifle and deflected it toward the wall. To his surprise as much as mine, my weapon discharged into the wall, and before I could swing it back around in his direction, he tackled me down the stairs.

We tumbled down the staircase in a mess of tangled limbs and fell sprawled out at the bottom. I tried to get up but he was up and on top of me like a dog. I tried to scurry away from under him as he had removed his helmet and began pummeling me with it. I continued to attempt to shimmy across the floor, all the while protecting my face from his blows with my arm. When I had shuffled my way down the hall to the front door with the German still on top of me, I made another attempt to get to my feet. Using the wall beside the door I began to prop myself up with my back before he took me down with another tackle. This time it sent us both spilling through the door and out onto the snow. There, I continued to struggle, doing all I could to simply protect myself from the constant battering of his helmet.

Then, to my bemusement, he stopped.

I brought my arms away from my face to see he was looking away. Following his gaze, I spotted what he was looking at.

To the north, on the ridge of the tree line, was a German tank followed by at least fifteen riflemen. I thought I was finished. Surely he would signal them over and that would be the end of me. But instead of calling for support, the German, who had taken me by surprise and overpowered me with his physical superiority, scurried to his feet and took off in the other direction. In a dazed confusion, I watched him go.

When I looked back to the German tank, its cannon began to swivel toward me and I, too, lunged to my feet and took off for the opposing trees. I heard the blast of the tank, then the eruption of the farm house behind me. I was showered with splinters of wood as I zig-zagged through the open field. I spotted the German ahead of me and chose to follow. The ground to my left erupted in a geyser of dirt and snow and I felt the ground beneath me toss me into the air. I landed on my feet and kept on running. Perhaps all those grueling runs in training were finally paying off. I burst into the trees behind the German without thought or reason, then I ran some more.

Three

The Germans were still in pursuit—of this I was sure. One misstep and I would most certainly be done for. I scanned the snowy ground in front of me as I ran, making sure not to trip over any exposed tree roots or fallen branches. I was catching up to the German from the farm house. Though he overpowered me in physical strength, I seemed to be the better runner. Once I had matched his pace, I signaled for us to go right in an attempt to lose the infantry's sight-line in the dense trees. He shook his head and kept on forward. For reasons I am still unsure of, I reached out and grabbed him by the collar of his olive, almost grey uniform and yanked him in my direction. Momentarily, he lost his footing in the slippery snow but regained his posture without breaking his stride and we went right.

Up ahead I could see orange flames glowing through the low-hanging fog that crept through the woods omi-nously like smoke from a witch's bubbling cauldron. The trees around us spat bark into the air as the incoming gunfire caused small explosions up and down their trunks. Continuing through the pines, I could now see the source of the flames. Stationed within the dreary, snow-covered woods was a British tank, blackened from burning, with flames spewing from somewhere within its left tread. I pointed to it, and this time the German seemed to agree with my direction.

We scampered over to the tank, snow flinging from our heels, and climbed aboard the side that was not alight. The metal of the tank was still excruciatingly hot, even if the fire that had recently fully encompassed it had mostly burnt out. The flesh on my numb hands sizzled as I pulled myself up but I was not deterred. Once on top of the tread, I began to slide as the bottom of my boots melted.

The top hatch was open and I clambered inside with the German following suit right after me.

The inside of the tank was like an oven. The heat made it hard to breathe, but what was worse was the smell. The average British tank needed four men to operate efficiently in combat, there were three inside of this one.

I reached out my burnt hands and threw one of the charred British corpses down to the bottom of the cramped hull. The German grabbed the other two and did the same. With the three stiffened and black corpses relocated to the bottom of the hull, we lay down on top of them to protect ourselves from the screaming hot metal of the floor.

Two thoughts briefly rattled through my mind as I lay there, shoulder to shoulder with my enemy on top of the burnt bodies of my allies. One was my footprints. They would lead them right to us in the snow like guide markers, but often in a situation like the one those German infantrymen had found themselves in—where the people they were after could be hidden behind any tree waiting to respond with gunfire of their own—the ground is the last place the eye wanders to, or so I had hoped. And the second thought was the heat. I had just gone from one blistering extreme to the other. The immense heat inside this tank wasn't just thawing out my frozen body, it was cooking me alive.

"It's too hot!" muttered the German.

"Shut up!" I hissed back at him, trying to listen for the pursuing German unit approaching over top of the wheezing whine of roasted flesh beneath me.

"I can't!" said the German and he began to rise when again I grabbed him by his sleeve and held him down.

"Now I don't know why a Kraut like you is running away from your own damn kind, but I wouldn't much like them finding me neither."

Sweat ran down his face, cutting channels like rivers in the dirt of his cheeks.

"If we can handle weeks of cold, we can handle fifteen minutes of heat. Now shut the fuck up."

I let go of his uniform with a shove and he buried his face in his hands.

After maybe four more minutes like that, I couldn't handle the heat any longer either. I tried to withstand it out of sheer stubbornness but he was right. It *was* too hot in there. Reluctantly, I gave the German the OK to evacuate.

We poured out of the top of the tank like chimney smoke and jumped down onto the dry snow. The brief moment of relief was quickly snatched away by the frigid wind that ripped through my uniform like knives. The sweat that now covered my body felt as if it froze the very instant of my leaving that hatch. I crawled, as I was trained to, under the tank and into the open cavity between its two treads to get out of sight in case the pursuing Germans were still advancing on us. This time my German companion did not follow. I turned to look for him to find him casually sat up against a tree, exhausted. I gestured for him to join me under the tank using hand signals but he shook his head. I dismissed this with some frustration, turned back around on my belly, retrieved my rifle from my back and lay prone, ready to defend myself.

After ten or so minutes, the crunching sound of footsteps pulled my attention back toward where the German had been sitting to see him walking away into the trees. I almost called after him before wisely deciding against it. My brow lowered, my lips pursed, and my nose flared but there was nothing I could do for him now. It was his funeral, I guessed.

I shuffled back around in the snow with my rifle forward, ready for the pursuing unit, but could not stop thinking about the German. *The enemy.* The one who had beat the shit out of me, then run from his own men, and was now simply walking away into the woods.

I put my focus back in front of me again and for a moment it was like I was right back in my fox hole, south of Foy. Right back to the place I had so cowardly run away from. I lowered my rifle.

Crawling backward, I emerged from the underbelly of that burnt-out British tank, rose to my feet, and began walking after the German through the snow. He turned to see me coming and waited for me to catch up.

Four

We walked in silence for a time as the snow began to fall once again through the trees as it had done since the day I arrived in Belgium. It was nice being with someone again, regardless of our opposing nationalities. I had been alone for six days in those frozen woods since leaving my fox hole, and the presence of life amongst all the death I had come across was welcome.

"What's your name?" I asked, my breath visible in the cool afternoon air.

He turned to me as if startled by my voice but did not respond.

"Come on, I know you know English."

"Strauss."

"Is that your first name or your last name?"

"Dieter Von Strauss is my full name," he replied with his eyes to the snowy ground in front of him.

"Well, Mr. Strauss, my name is Henry. Henry Gerald Briggs."

He nodded to me in a seemingly friendly enough way. It was more like a small bow of the head than a nod of agreement. I continued.

"Growing up it was Gerald Henry Briggs. I always went by Gerry. Seems like a bit of an oversight on my father's part, being that they called your kind *Jerrys* during the first war. Still do, I guess. That's why I enlisted using my middle name as my first. Does that make sense?" I could hear myself rambling. I had no idea how to carry on a conversation with a German—let alone anyone I didn't know—but I was trying, however awkward and incoherent I knew I sounded. Then we were silent again.

"You hit pretty hard, you know?" I said, talking more out of unease than anything else, though this brought a smirk to the German's face. Seeing I had gotten a reaction, I decided to pursue this topic further. "Throwing your gun at me on the stairs was a dirty move, by the way. They teach you that in training?"

His smirk widened across his thin face. "That was the first time I had fired that weapon," he said, his accent thick.

"Yeah? Well, it looks like it was the last time, as well. Look at you, no helmet, no gun. What kind of German soldier are you?" I was trying to keep it light, almost playful.

"I am not a soldier," he replied. "I am merely a translator." His smile began to fade.

"So, what's that? You tell the Krauts what we're saying?"

"Precisely."

"OK," I nodded. "You know what cocksucker means?" I asked with a goofy grin on my face.

"I am not familiar with this word."

"Really? Never heard it before?"

"No."

"I'll teach you. How old are you anyway?"

"Seventeen."

This reminded me of Eugene, but I put that out of my mind like I had been trying to for the last several weeks.

"Seventeen, huh? Well that's way too young to know a word like that," I jested, but I don't believe he understood my humor.

"I'm plenty old enough," he responded, straightening up, broadening his shoulders.

"OK, well, when is your birthday?" I asked.

"January 22."

"All right, Mr. Strauss. You ask me again on your birthday and I'll tell you what it means."

I think recognizing the prospect of us surviving another few weeks filled him with a kind of hope as his smile returned and he nodded in agreement.

"How long have you been fighting for?" I asked him.

"A year."

"You've been out here a year?"

"Yes."

"So, you were sixteen when you joined?"

"Yes."

"Gee, those Germans recruit them young, don't they?"

"I suppose."

"Did they even ask you your age?"

"I told them I was sixteen and they said I better go outside and celebrate a few birthdays before coming back in."

"Wow." My eyebrows shot high on my forehead. "So you wanted to fight?"

"No, though I could speak your language and I was told that was valuable."

"And you never fired your weapon that whole time?"

"I had, just not *that* weapon. *That* weapon was given to me."

"What, you some kind of war hero or something?"

Though his face was white with cold, I could see his cheeks reddening.

"I'd rather not speak about it."

Damn, it seemed as if I had overstepped. "OK, we don't have to talk about it."

The silence returned.

"Do you know where we're going?" I asked.

"Generally, yes."

"OK," I said without protest or indifference.

"You're shivering," I said as the sun began to fade from the cloudy sky.

"It's cold," Dieter replied with his arms crossed over his chest.

"You want to wear my helmet?" I asked him.

He looked at me, confused. "Why would you give me your helmet?"

"Well, seeing as you no longer have a weapon, I don't have to worry about you popping me in the head when

I'm not looking. And also, you lose 40 to 45 percent of your body heat through your head. I read that somewhere." I unclipped my chinstrap and slid the helmet from my head and offered it to him. I could feel my greasy hair flattened against my scalp as it remained stationary in the gentle breeze.

Dieter accepted it with some skepticism and looked it over. I mimed putting it over my head with my hands and he did so, leaving the chinstrap unbuckled and hanging loosely on either side of his face.

"It's very large," he said, surprised.

"You saying I got a big head?" I joked.

"No, it's just bigger than mine was."

Again, he didn't grasp my attempt at humor.

"Dank Schön," he said, with sincerity in his voice.

"What does that mean?" I asked.

"Thank you."

My lips rose into a warm smile and I nodded.

When nightfall inevitably came, we stumbled upon three naked men, lying side by side in the snow, face down. I walked over to examine the bodies. When I approached, a mischief of rats, who had been feasting on the fingers and toes of these unfortunate souls, scurried away into the trees. One birthed itself from one of the men's rectums and joined the rest. There were signs of real mischief indeed.

In the napes of the necks of all three men, a spent cartridge had been driven into their spines. This was a trick picked up by the German's from the Russian's during the early stages of the war. How one conceives of such savagery is beyond me. We kept on.

It was nearly pitch black when we came across a tree, uprooted from the ground and on its side in the snow. Its limbless trunk offered little protection from the conditions, so we gathered branches and leaned them up against the tree's fallen base. Once satisfied we crawled into our makeshift shelter and huddled together for warmth.

By first light, we were on the move again, but soon I needed to stop as the pain in my feet was too great.

"I need to sit down," I said, and plopped my butt down into the snow.

"What is the issue?" Dieter asked.

"It's my feet. I just need a couple minutes."

Dieter then kneeled down in front of me and began untying my boots.

"Hey, hey, hey," I said, waving him away.

He looked at me undeterred.

"When was the last time you had your boots off?" he asked, still on one knee.

"Weeks, maybe," I replied.

"You need to take them off," he said and began working at the knots in my laces again.

This time I let him, figuring he probably had more experience with this kind of thing than I.

With a great deal of pain, Dieter slid my boots from my feet before peeling my socks off as well. I was afraid to look. I knew it couldn't be good, but my curiosity got the better of me.

When I finally looked down at my bare feet, they were wrinkled beyond belief and bore a greyish/ blue complexion. The tips of my toes had gone black, a black that seemed to be crawling up my foot.

"Goddammit," I said aloud and turned my head away in disgust.

"We need a fire," said Dieter with one of my wrinkled feet in his hands.

"No fire. It could give away our position."

Dieter looked around the foggy woods and said, "I can barely see the trees twenty yards away. I don't think anyone will see it."

I shook my head. "We can't risk it."

And now, for the first time since our paths had unexpectedly intertwined, Dieter seemed to take command.

"You're going to lose your feet if we don't. We have no other option."

With this, he began gathering sticks and twigs in the immediate area. Seeing his immediacy filled me with an anxiety I had been trying to avoid. I too began grasping at twigs in the snow around me.

When Dieter returned, he had two handfuls of pencil-thin sticks of wood, as well as a branch, with the length of about eight feet and the width of a wrist, dragging behind him, under his arm. He removed the helmet I had given him, placed it in the snow upside down, and unloaded his haul of sticks inside it like pasta into a pot of boiling water. He then took the eight-foot branch and began swinging it into the trunk of a tree like a baseball bat. This caused the branch to snap at the point of contact. He continued doing this until the entire branch had been broken down into one-foot sections.

He placed three of these sections into the snow as a base for the fire and ran off into the white fog once again. I watched in amazement at the calculated efficiency of this boy.

When he returned, he had a fistful of white birch bark. He began tearing the thin sheets into strips before gathering it all into his hands and rubbing them together feverishly. Now satisfied with his preparation, he placed the ball of thinly peeled birch bark on top of the branches he had laid in the snow and retrieved a lighter from his pocket. The birch bark caught almost instantly, and he grabbed a handful of smaller twigs from the upturned helmet and fed the small bundle to the building flame, but the twigs refused to light.

"Too wet," he muttered in frustration, but kept at it.

Soon the twigs caught and a delicate flame of about five inches rose promisingly. He then retrieved the remaining sticks from the helmet and placed them on top of the flame at an opposing angle.

Due to the moisture held within the wood, great plumes of smoke rose into the air, and this worried me. Now Dieter was placing the larger pieces of the branch he had processed over the burning twigs and a healthy fire began to burn.

"Dry your socks and boots. Warm your feet," he said, and before I could answer, off he went back into the trees for more firewood.

The warmth of the fire almost produced an emotional response within me. I huddled around it and graciously accepted its heat. My feet began to throb as they unthawed by the fire, but the pain was overshadowed by a sense of primitive joy that I hadn't felt in some time.

I hung my soggy socks over the toes of my boots and stationed them just beside the fire in the snow. Soon they were steaming.

Dieter came back with a great amount of long and twisting branches that he had looped his arms around and dragged behind him. Again, he swung them at the trunk of a tree and gathered the processed wood into a pile beside me. Then he knelt across from me, huffing and puffing, and fed a few more logs into the fire.

"How are your feet?" he asked, grabbing a handful of snow and rubbing his face with it.

"Warm," I said, and for some reason I began to laugh as if I had just delivered the punchline of a hilarious joke.

"Warm is good!" Dieter responded and joined me in roaring, child-like laughter.

"Good idea with the birch bark," I said with my hands outstretched toward the flames.

"You know birch bark?" he replied, finding my knowledge of natural fire starters curious.

"I grew up on a farm. Birch bark is great for starting a fire."

"I was surprised to find it," he replied. "These woods are pine plantations—I was lucky."

"Amen to that," I replied and held my hand out to him. Understanding my meaning, he leaned forward and planted his hand against mine and high-fived me and we enjoyed the warmth of the fire together.

Five

After nearly an hour by the fire, it had sunk into the snow down to the grass below in a perfect blackened circle. The warmth had been an incredible boost to my morale and I dreaded the thought of having to move on.

"We'll have to stop every few hours to dry your feet," said Dieter through the column of smoke that rose between us.

"I will be OK," I replied.

"Ah, stubborn Amerikaner." Dieter took my helmet from the snow and placed it back onto his head. "Will you trust me?" he asked.

I nodded my head. "Yeah, OK."

Dieter picked up my boots and slid his hand inside them. "They are dry now. Time to go."

Gently, he handed them to me and I accepted them as if they were an ancestral gift. They were warm as I put them on.

Dieter rose to his feet and offered his hand. I took it and he helped me to mine. Once up, I joined him in kicking snow onto the fire that hissed in protest. Then we moved onward into the lazy hanging fog of the woods.

Around noon we stumbled onto the stale remnants of a battlefield. The dead lay crooked in the snow where they had fallen. Both German and American men dotted the landscape with weapons still clenched within frozen fingers. Surveying the carnage was eerie in its absolute stillness. You could even hear birds singing in the snow-covered trees.

There was no getting used to seeing men in this way. You hoped you would for the sake of your own mental preservation, but the sight of human beings ripped apart and so impossibly mutilated on such an unimaginable scale always positioned you on the edge of madness.

"We should check them for supplies," said Dieter, scanning the battlefield.

Softly, I closed my eyes, finding the proposition revolting, however necessary.

The closest body to me was that of a German soldier. I walked over to him and began patting the pockets of his jacket.

"You check your men, I'll check mine," said Dieter.

By his tone, it sounded as if by searching the fallen German had offended him.

I sprang to my feet. "Yeah, of course."

Dieter took my position overtop of the dead German and continued the search I had begun.

I sauntered over through the trees where the Americans lay with tense muscles, feeling I had upset my German companion before once again patting down pockets.

The Americans proved to not be carrying much at all. A few squares of Hershey's chocolate, a couple extra magazines of ammunition for my 1911, and a lot of wet clothes. Some men, however, had wool gloves in their pockets, as well as wool caps on their heads and wool socks on their cold feet. One man, possibly a captain, wore a long overcoat that I struggled to remove from his stiff arms.

Was I in a better position than I had been before finding these men? Yes. But I did not feel good about it.

In the case of one man, I had stripped him down to his stained briefs.

When all was said and done I walked back over to the German side of the battlefield to see how Dieter was making out with the soldier's uniform draped over my forearm. He was still searching as there had been more German dead than American.

I approached him, hunched over one of his men. "Find anything?" I asked.

"Some bread, some Wurst, enough." He looked as equally displeased about what we were doing as I did.

"Good. Here." I held out my arm with the American uniform slung over it.

He looked at it, confused. "What am I to do with this?" he asked.

"Wear it. By my estimation we're walking into Allied territory. They'll shoot you on sight wearing what you have on now."

I could see the wheels turning in his head. "And if we run into Germans?" he asked, curiously.

"Then we're both dead," I replied. "Put it on."

With some disdain, he obliged.

I handed him a pair of gloves as well as one of the woolen caps I had managed to find. He put them on, as well.

"They're wet," he protested.

"Then we better get a fire on soon, but not here."

He nodded back to me.

"Nice coat," he added.

"I think it's a captain's coat. If we come across any Allied forces, I may be able to talk our way out of it now."

Again, he nodded, though I could see he wasn't entirely sold on my reasoning.

"I'm ready to leave when you are," he said to me, slinging the American uniform over his bare shoulders.

"OK, let's go."

Together, we walked away from the gruesome scene, not looking back.

Our second fire went a lot more smoothly than the first. We leisurely gathered our fire materials without the frantic rush we felt before.

On sticks shoved into the snow hung over the fire limply the items of clothing we had scavenged from our fallen men. Dieter had placed the few slices of rye bread he had managed to gather on a hot bed of coals to toast beside the stale Wurst sausages he had also been fortunate enough to find. We ate in a state of primal ecstasy. The sausage burnt the insides of our mouths as we jostled our heads from left to right with mouths agape, venting steam, as one does when trying to redistribute something too hot to eat.

I told Dieter he looked good in an American uniform and he said his father would surely kill him if he saw him wearing it. We continued to eat in silence entirely focused on our meals.

"Yesterday," I began, "you said you had a general idea about where you were going when you left me under that tank."

Dieter looked up to me from the toast in his hand.

"I did."

"Just where is it you're trying to get to?"

He balanced the half-eaten slice of toast on his knee and wiped the crumbs from his hands into the fire. "Chenogne," he muttered, almost under his breath.

"What the hell is in Chenogne?" I asked.

"It does not matter," he replied, his face gone red.

"Come on," I pried. "I think I can say we're friends now, are we not? Friends tell each other things."

He looked down to the slice of toasted rye bread on his knee the way a child looks away from a camera in shyness. "A woman," he said at last.

"A woman?" I hollered. "You deserted your men for a woman?"

"I did not desert!" he fired back, his spine stiffening.

"OK, OK, you did not desert." I waved a hand of dismissal. "Forget I said that."

Dieter simmered down and began eating his toast again. An awkwardness hung in the air briefly.

"What's her name?" I asked, trying to lighten things up again.

"Patty," he replied after swallowing.

"That's not a very German name."

"That is because she is not German."

"Well, where is she from? Is she Belgium? Belgish? I'm not sure how you say it."

"It's Belgian. And, no, she's American."

I slumped back, jutting my chin into my chest in surprise. "She's American?"

"Is this not what I said?" I believe he was trying to come off as arrogant but I could tell he was more flustered with embarrassment.

"Well, I'll be. A German soldier falling in love with an American dame. I can't think of a better love story."

"*Ha, ha,*" he said with a monotone delivery.

"How is that even possible? What the hell is an American broad doing all the way over here?"

"She was traveling when the war broke out. She has been stuck here ever since."

"Well, she must have been stuck here for years then."

"Yes," Dieter replied.

Wow, I thought to myself. *I wonder what her story is.*

"How old is she?" I asked, seeing that he seemed unnecessarily reserved.

"Twenty-seven."

"Oh, you absolute dog!" I hollered, and leaned over and shoved him. This had him laughing, regardless of how hard he was trying to hide it.

"So that makes her, what, ten years older than you?!" My excitement seemed to liven him up a bit.

"I suppose."

"What do you mean *I suppose?*" I imitated, in my best German accent, which wasn't all that good.

He began to chuckle. His shoulders bounced up and down.

"I suppose that means she is!"

Now we were both laughing.

"That is unbelievable!" I cried, completely forgetting that at any moment we could be heard and executed by either side.

Dieter continued to chuckle while giving me a "What can you do?" expression.

"So, you guys must have . . . you know."

"Oh, yes," he replied in such a confident and matter-of-fact tone that it had me in stitches.

I was howling with laughter, which soon spread to Dieter. It was something that I had not experienced in a long, long time, and I cherished every second of it.

"You know what? You're something else, you know that?" I said as my braying began to wind down.

Dieter leaned over and gave me a playful jab to the shoulder. I knew right then and there that Dieter had a brother because he knew just the right spot to hit you and have it hurt.

Six

"Tell me again what she looks like," I said as we trudged through the snow as the sun began to lower in the white-washed skies above.

"No, I don't think I will." He gave me a snobby grin.

"Ah, you cocksucker."

Dieter turned to me, curious. "So this word. It is an insult?"

"Yeah," I replied. "I mean, it can be."

"Stop right there!" A male voice barked out from behind us. Both Dieter and I froze. I glanced over to him without moving my head and he looked back with equally panicked eyes.

I began to turn my body toward the voice that had emerged from behind us.

"Don't!" he commanded and I turned back away from him.

"Are either one of you a medic?" the voice asked, now sounding weak and desperate.

I let out a sigh of relief.

"No," I replied.

"Do you have any morphine?" the voice asked.

Before I could answer, Dieter responded. "I do."

"Give it to me."

"OK," replied Dieter. "I'm going to turn around now and give it to you."

Dieter began to turn.

"Keep looking forward!" the voice demanded, now shrill in cadence. Dieter did as he asked.

"Hold it out and I will retrieve it," said the voice and I could hear his footsteps walking toward us, crunching the frozen top layer of snow.

Dieter rummaged through the first aid pouch on his waist and removed the syringe of morphine. "Are you hurt?" he asked.

"This is not your concern," replied the voice, closer now.

Dieter held the syringe in his hand, which was out to his side between us. "Just take it," he said, and the man continued toward us.

What happened next I did not expect. In the blink of an eye, Dieter grabbed the man by his extended arm and twisted it with the twirl of his body. The man yelped as he was thrown to the ground. I drew my 1911 and fixed it on the man as he scampered in the snow, trying to get back up. Dieter then kicked the man in the hand, seeing that it held a firearm, which was sent far into the trees. When the man managed to get onto his back, I had him at gunpoint.

He looked to be a man in his late forties with grey beginning to pepper the chin of his dark beard. He was in civilian clothes and held his open palms toward us.

"OK, wait, wait," he mumbled in a softer tone than you would expect for someone pleading for their life. "Please, don't. I just need help. My son. My son!"

I looked over to Dieter who had gone to fetch the man's pistol. When he returned, he presented the weapon to me by the handle. Engraved in the wooden handle was a red number nine.

"It's a red nine," he said, before turning to the man in the snow. "Where did you get this?" He asked him.

"I've had it since the Great War." The man replied.

"You fought for Germany?"

"*Ja,*" replied the man.

"Lower your weapon," Dieter said to me.

"Are you crazy?" I began, but Dieter took his hand and rested it on the top of my sidearm and gently pushed it away.

"Your son, you said. Is he hurt?" Dieter asked the man.

"He is."

"Show me."

The man slowly rose to his feet and waved us in his direction.

I looked to Dieter as if to say, "I don't like this," but Dieter turned and walked after the man.

I holstered my weapon and followed suit.

After twenty minutes of walking, we came upon a cave in a shallow rocky hillside. The entrance had been crudely fitted with wood-framed single pane windows and a simple door. I could see the dirty faces of wide-eyed children peering out through the murky windows like tourists on a bus marveling at the sights of a foreign city.

"How many people are in there?" I asked as we approached.

"Four other families, not including my own," the man replied.

"And you all live here?"

"Our homes were destroyed in the bombings. We had nowhere else to go." He walked up to the door that had been framed right into the stone entrance of the cave and held it open, waiting for us to follow. I stopped and looked to Dieter with worry in my eyes. Dieter simply nodded his head in response.

I sighed in contempt and followed them both inside.

The inside of the cave struck me first as primitive, though as my eyes adjusted to the sudden dark I began to see modern beds and dark wooden dressers along the cave walls. In the center sat an unlit fire pit, grey with ash, with a contraption overtop of it constructed from branches on which two cast-iron pots hung. Beside this was a healthy pile of firewood and a stack of bricks that rose all the way to the roof of the cave. I assumed this to be some kind of support column.

The next thing I began to notice was the children. There must have been twelve kids, all under the age of ten, huddled up against their parents' legs in fear of us with dark marbles for eyes.

"Where is your boy?" asked Dieter.

"Right this way."

Now, not only the children's eyes, but the eyes of all of the cave occupants followed us as we were led deeper inside, their clothes, ragged and soiled with filth, hung loosely from their famished bodies.

Through a narrow passage that dripped with condensation was a small dwelling. Two beds rested up against the stone of the cave wall, and in one of them a child lay motionless.

The man who had brought us there rushed to his bedside where a woman knelt with the boy's hand in hers.

He muttered something in German to her and she said something back.

The bed was slick with blood.

Dieter approached and began speaking German as well, which seemingly stunned the couple. For all they knew he was an American based on his pillaged uniform, but they continued speaking in their native tongue.

I stood, anxious and useless, and merely observed.

The woman pointed to the wound on the boy's body. In the shallow dip between the shoulder and the collarbone was the unmistakable entry wound of a bullet. Dieter retrieved a pouch of Sulfa powder and poured it into the wound; all the while, the boy lay unconscious, as pale as the winter moon. Dieter then brought his ear to the boy's mouth to listen to his breathing, then turned the boy to look for an exit wound, finding none.

The boy's father looked hollow in the face and stricken with worry, but the woman—whom I assumed to be the mother—seemed to be entirely drained of emotion.

They conversed again in German before Dieter began dressing the wound.

There is too much blood, I thought and lowered my head. Dieter placed his hand atop the mother's, who still held the hand of her child on the bed, then got up and walked over to me.

"I don't think he is going to make it," he whispered to me and I nodded, finding it hard to look at the boy. "They say we can stay until he's better."

"I thought you said he wasn't going to make it?" I replied. "I know."

Dieter walked back over to the couple, again saying something I didn't understand, and the father pointed to the far wall of the cave. Dieter shook his hand and walked back over to me.

"We can rest over here," he said, gesturing to the small dip in the wall.

"OK," I said, and joined him in sitting down.

"What are you thinking?" I asked Dieter over the distant crackle of the fire that had been lit a half hour before. Its flickering light danced along the rigid walls of stone and half covered Dieter's face in wavering shadow. Dieter gazed idly at the boy on the bed.

"He'll pass in the night. He's lost too much blood."

"Then what?"

"Then we move on, I guess."

I let out a long sigh and the father of the boy turned to face me, hearing my disgruntled expulsion of air. I shifted my eyes away from his like a schoolboy in trouble.

"How do you think it happened?" I asked Dieter under my breath.

"They figure a stray bullet," he replied.

"Christ."

"Americans did this," said Dieter coldly.

"Anyone could have shot that bullet," I replied.

"Not the bullet, the bombings. You see yourselves as conquerors, but all they see is destruction."

I shot Dieter a queer glance. "What alternative were we given?" I fired back, somewhat offended by his remarks.

"It is not your fault or mine," he said, seeing my frustration. "We are soldiers. We are told what to do and what direction to point our guns and shoot. All we are is just pieces on a board trying to keep our king from falling. I was told I was a hero and a patriot, just the same as I am sure you were."

"And just what point are you trying to make?" I asked him.

"Look at the boy on that bed. As we see it, Americans did that. Now, I have been fortunate. I have met Americans, I have even fallen in love with one. I know you not to be the fierce savages my country makes you out to be. Your men aren't all that different from my own." Dieter tilted his head back against the hard stone wall. "All I am saying is that I see all this fighting now as nothing more than theatre. Politics. My life means nothing to my country. I had become so caught up in it all. The information I was fed was so infuriating. But look at that boy—that is the only thing that comes from all this senseless fighting."

Dieter's words were as poetic as they were powerful.

"Earlier you called me a deserter," he continued, putting his eyes back on the boy. "Well, that may be true. But I simply could not fight another man's war any longer."

I could not find any words to respond. I had quit fighting out of fear and cowardice. He, on the other hand, had quit on principle. He may have only been seventeen but he had the heart of a man. This had me stupefied in my admiration.

When I turned to say something to him, his eyes were closed and his head drooped toward his chest. I decided to do the same, though sleep didn't find me as easily.

I woke from a swift kick to the thigh. When my eyes jolted open, the father of the boy was over top of me with tears and anger in his eyes. I attempted to get to my feet but was shoved back against the hard stone wall, crumbling back onto my rear end. Dieter, who had managed to rise, was trying to calm the man down in German, but he seemed inconsolable. He thrashed his arms and screamed at us. I looked over to the bed where the boy lay to see his limp head cradled in his mother's arms. A pit formed in the hollows of my belly.

I got to my feet as Dieter interacted with the hysterical man.

"We should go," I muttered, more to myself than to Dieter. I don't believe he heard me over the father's shrill cries. The father turned to me and shoved me again and I stumbled backward but remained on my feet.

"We should go!" I repeated, louder this time, my voice reverberating throughout the dark cave.

45

Dieter waved a hand toward me as if he felt he could get the situation under control, but as he did so, the father of the boy brandished a knife. Instinctively, I raised my weapon.

Now Dieter had both hands raised, one to me and the other to the boy's father.

"Henry, put that away," he said, in a calm and calculated voice.

"Not until he drops the knife," I responded.

The man, with the knife out in front of him, began inching forward, shouting in German, his face contorted as spit sprayed from his mouth in stringy globs. Now I addressed him directly. "Drop the knife!"

I heard a choir of yelling and cries as some of the families began to gather by the narrow passage behind me. This was getting out of control. I couldn't think, I couldn't move. Voices seemed to be shouting at me from all directions as they bounced from wall to wall. That is when the man lunged and I discharged my weapon.

The flash of my muzzle was like a lightning strike within the damp cave. An after image of the man's twisted face burned onto my retinas and the sound of the gunshot was deafening. Then the screaming erupted. Beyond the smoking barrel of my pistol, I watched as the mother of the boy collapsed over top of the man of which I had just shot as she clutched him in her arms. She wailed as he lay stunned on the ground, blood oozing from his chest. I turned and began pointing my weapon from one person to the next as they tried to rush in through the narrow passage. The children cried.

A shove came in from behind, and when I turned back to see who had pushed me, the mother of the boy was in my face, throwing her arms against me. The look in her eyes sent ice through my veins.

She continued to push and I was helpless to stop her. She pushed me back through the narrow passage and into the larger living quarters of the cave where the other families had begun hurling things at me. I was so overwhelmed that my brain simply refused to function. Dieter grabbed me by my arms and pulled me toward the door. The shouting continued.

Before I knew it, I was back out into the bright light of the day that was only intensified by the white snow that covered everything.

"I'm . . . I'm sorry," I heard myself mumble as Dieter dragged me along.

The last glance I had of the cave was of its occupants crowded in the door and by the windows.

"I'm sorry," I repeated so low there was no way they could have heard me. I was then turned around and marched through the snow with my eyes to the ground.

Seven

We walked in relative silence for most of the wretched day. The wind bit into the flesh of your face like passing razor blades and the snow on the ground must have risen a few inches as flurries cut across the trees sideways. It was late afternoon when we stopped to start a fire.

My hands trembled as I looked upon them, illuminated in the orange glow of the fire. I tried to convince myself it was from the cold or perhaps from the weakness of a starving body, but I knew it was really my nerves that were frayed from the events of the morning.

Dieter had filled his helmet with snow and rested it on the open flame to boil for drinking water. I could tell he was as saddened about what had transpired as I was. No conversation was needed to convey that point. Instead we sat with our steaming socks hung over the fire and nibbled on the little rations of rye and Wurst we had left, though neither of us felt like eating despite our grumbling stomachs.

"We should think about a shelter early if the snow keeps up this way," said Dieter.

I stared blankly into the dancing flames and nodded idly.

"It happened," Dieter asserted definitively. "There's nothing you can do about it now."

My eyes shifted up toward his. "Would you have done the same?" I asked.

"The way I see it, he gave you no choice."

I relived the moment in my head, chewing the dead skin on my lower lip. It peeled off in strips. "What was he saying?" I asked him.

"You're just torturing yourself."

"What did he say?" For the first time since our standoff on the staircase, I raised my voice to Dieter.

Dieter seemed to deflate, as if finding that being forced to relive that moment as well brought him great pain.

"He grieved," he said. "He was grieving. He blamed us. He was upset and irrational."

I spat a strip of dead skin that clung to my tongue. I tasted blood in my mouth. We sat in silence for a moment before Dieter got to his feet.

"Come on, help me find some stuff for a shelter."

I did as he asked.

The night was miserable. We ran out of wood for the fire in the early hours of the morning and clung to each other, shivering, for what felt like an eternity.

For the next several days we walked like automatons. The only process our famished minds executed was summoning one foot to proceed the other. We came across a family unit of deer sitting together by the base of a tree, their bodies covered in a light layer of snow. It never occurred to me how deer shelter themselves from the elements. Most smaller animals of the woods, such as rabbits and foxes, burrow into the ground for protection. Even bigger animals such as bears dig dens. But as it appeared to us then, deer simply sit down and endure it. We admired their resilience as well as envied it.

We tried to shoot one, of course, but the shot went high and they scattered into the thick fog and vanished like ghostly apparitions.

After much protest, Dieter convinced me that we could no longer continue in the woods if we wanted to survive. We would have to look for a village, or some sign of civilization, to get out of this cold. As much as the prospect of leaving the protection of these formidable woods—a place for which I had developed a strange fondness regardless of their nearly inhospitable conditions—frightened me, I knew he was right.

It was then we began to journey outward from the dense heart of these misty woodlands. In truth we had no bearing on any semblance of direction. The sun had become so diffused by the clouds and fog that everything seemed to be lit evenly, giving us no hope of guidance. But still, we pressed on.

As a boy, I was raised Catholic. I would join my family in thanking God every night for the food on our plates and I attended church every Sunday. Though in war, it was hard to believe in such a loving creator. In just my short time here, in this hellish icebox known as Belgium, I had seen things that shook my fragile beliefs. What god would allow such savagery to occur? What god would idly watch his creatures tear each other apart to capture a mere mile of ground? What god would have created such a cruel and evil force to oppose us? These questions lingered in my mind like a fire on the horizon, crawling forward on its fat belly like a beast to consume everything it crossed. Could there be such a god?

The weather was much worse than it had been the day before. What was once a droning flurry had become a violent blizzard. It forced us to walk backward to the wind, as to walk against it was like standing in front of a sand blaster to any exposed flesh. The falling snow felt hard and sharp against the skin, like millions of little spearheads hurtled through the air.

By midday, we attempted to light a fire but the winds were too strong. We knelt, hunched over the lighter, but it was of no use. We kept on.

I had never been so cold as I was that night. It was a cold that is almost indescribable. Those frozen nights near Foy were no tropical paradise but compared to this they seemed mild and tolerable. Nothing seemed to have any feeling; my hands were the color of driftwood, and if I felt so obliged to slit my own throat and end all this suffering, not a drop of blood would drip from my frozen veins.

The following day was more of the same. The shivering was utterly uncontrollable and I could feel small chips of broken teeth on my tongue from the constant chattering of my jaw.

How was it possible to be so cold?

Dieter seemed to be in just as bad a state as me. His face looked red and raw. His eyelashes were coated in a layer of frost, as well as the rims of his nostrils. Our bodies weren't even producing enough heat to deter snow from sticking to the very skin of our faces. I believe we both wished to die.

By the second night in this horrendous storm, I had broken down completely. My tears froze to my eyelids as soon as my eyes could produce them and this yielded a great pain. I couldn't help but think about all the times I had simply worn a T-shirt outside and been completely comfortable with my bare arms exposed. Or going to bed naked without bedding with a wet cloth on my chest because it was too hot to sleep in those Pennsylvania summers. I thought about warm baths and burning my fingers on a cigarette I refused to extinguish before I had *just one more puff.* I don't know how we survived that night. It seemed as if it were a nightmare of which my mind refuses to recollect, or perhaps it was in such a pure state of survival that recording those long hours of grueling punishment was considered irrelevant.

The third day, as if God Himself heard my earlier questionings about His role in all this, the snow stopped and the sky grew clear. I rose to my feet and joyously felt the sun's warmth on my face like a flower on the first day of spring. I began to cry once again but this time there was no pain or defeat in my heart.

Dieter and I hugged and jumped and howled with joy like feral beings, which in a way we were. As our bodies thawed, the pain returned, but this was easily disregarded in our ecstasy. We struck a fire and moaned like lovers in its heat.

OK, God, I see you.

Eight

When the fog had fully dispersed after about an hour, we turned to see that we were right near the tree line that exited the woods. If we had taken twenty more paces before hunkering down in the snow and covering ourselves with tree branches to try and rest we would have made it out of there before the moon kissed the sky. A short field lay just before us, bordered by a fence constructed of young tree trunks where the snow lay atop them thicker than the fence poles themselves, and, beyond that, a small village. It looked like something out of a fairy tale or perhaps an image that could have graced the front of a Christmas postcard. Without extinguishing our fire, we practically pranced for it, using a new-found energy neither of us knew we had.

The snow was much deeper on the other side of the woods, having been unprotected from the canopy cover the pine trees provided. We sank down to our kneecaps with every floundering step as we ran toward the village like children to an ice cream van in the middle of July and barged into the first house we came across. What greeted us when we burst through the door, probably looking like wild mountain men, were the stunned faces of a small family at their table who were enjoying breakfast before our sudden intrusion. Both Dieter and I, as well as this family of three—a mother, a father, and son of about six—were at a complete loss as to how to react, but to our surprise, it was the mother who made the first move by offering us a seat at the table. I was unsure if it was a gesture of kindness or of fear, but I graciously accepted.

You could feel the timidity in the air as we sat down and inched our chairs up to the table. The mood in the room felt delicate, as if one wrong misconstrued move-ment would cause the pleasant scene before us to erupt into chaos. But as if sensing this, the mother slid a plate of bread and cheese across the table toward us. I looked to her for reassurance and she nodded back with a faint smile on her face. Then, as if in a primal frenzy, both Dieter and I began scarfing down the contents of the plate with filthy fingers. Mouthfuls of warm, soft bread were followed up by cubes of strong cheese. I had to remind myself to chew as I sucked it all back like air.

The mother, stepping back to join her family on the other side of the table, simply watched as if we were animals in a zoo introduced to the feeding trough. Dieter reached for a glass jar of jam and brought it to his mouth like a cup of water. When his mouth overflowed with the sweet, crimson jam and it spilled from the sides, he handed it to me, and I did the same.

The contrast of the strong, almost bitter cheese and the sweetness of the jam was like nothing I had tasted before. Those flavors shouldn't have mixed as well as they did, but my starving body accepted them without protest. I think I would have begun eating the plate itself in my famished condition.

I glanced across the table to the family, who had huddled together and were observing us from a safe distance. A shot of guilt ran through my body. We had so rudely and abruptly barged into their home and quite literally taken the food from their table. My chewing slowed and I felt somewhat shameful in my careless indulgence. I looked down to the plate that was once so elegantly adorned with fresh bread slices and cubes of succulent cheeses that now looked so barbarically ravaged, and slapped Dieter on the chest. He nearly choked on his food before seemingly coming to the same selfish conclusion I had. He also stopped eating and our faces went red with childish embarrassment.

I slid the plate back across the table for this family, who had generously accepted us, to have some for themselves. The mother, whom I took for being extremely brave given the circumstances, waved a hand and suggested for us to continue eating and I waved my hand back.

"Please eat," I heard myself say, though it was obvious she didn't understand my language.

Dieter repeated what I had said in German, but it was clear she did not understand him either.

I pointed to the food on the table and then gestured with pinched fingers, moving them toward my mouth, then pointed to her and her family.

She gave me a small nod and brought the plate closer to her and they began to pick out what was left.

As I watched I licked the remnants of my meal from my cracked lips, feeling the rough fuzz of stubble on the tip of my tongue above my mouth. I hadn't realized just how much my beard had grown over these last few weeks, though Dieter's face remained smooth.

I started to get up to leave when the woman gestured for us to stay put in our chairs. She rushed off into a room with her night dress wavering behind her as she went. When she returned, her arms were full of folded clothes, the way one would carry firewood. She rounded the table and offered them to us with a gentle smile. I returned the look with as friendly a smile as I could muster on my rugged face and took a shirt, a pair of pants, underwear, and socks from the pile. She then motioned for us to remove our uniforms.

I don't believe Dieter or I had received such kindness in our entire time during the war, which for me wasn't admittedly that long. It felt almost as peculiar as enjoying warm, fresh food after weeks of cold, stale rations.

The woman then waved her hand in a "right this way" gesture. I rose from the table, as well as Dieter, and she guided us to a room I could only describe as "cozy," with our change of clothes in hand. Once she had closed the door, I turned to Dieter. We didn't need to say anything to understand what each other was thinking: *Can you believe this?*

We didn't seem to have any reluctance to remove all of our clothes in front of each other. The need to put on something dry and clean was too strong.

When Dieter removed his shirt, the presence of his protruding ribs and collarbones was shocking. Once I had my shirt off as well, I examined myself for the first time in weeks and saw that I too looked like a skeleton. The first thing I thought was that I looked like a beached thing. Not only my ribs, but my hip bones as well seemed to jut from my body in sharp and strange angles. It was as frightening as it was staggering.

After removing my boots and socks, I could see the blackness of my feet seemed to have spread. What was once blotches and spots that resembled something like mold, had solidified into a solid color. It looked as if I had dipped half my foot into a bucket of black paint.

I stepped into the pair of soft—presumably cotton—pants gingerly, and it felt as if I had wrapped myself in a blanket. Sliding the shirt over my bony shoulders had the same effect.

When we emerged back into the main room of the little log cabin, the woman was waiting for us to retrieve our mucky uniforms. She took them and again, whisked off to another part of the house.

We walked into what looked like a living room, where a brick fireplace sheltered a glorious fire.

On a couch made of wood and cloth sat the father and son. We nodded awkwardly and the father motioned for us to sit in front of the fire, which we did.

I lowered myself to the floor, which was covered with a thin floral rug, its corners curled upward from years in front of the fire's heat, and sat with my feet and hands to the flames. My eyes closed as if on their own and I basked in the warmth. Dieter had done the same.

The boy, who seemingly looked older now, somehow, came and sat beside us on the floor. His face was blank but friendly. He had a tuft of blonde hair that sat neatly on his small head and had eyes of the richest blue. We sat in silence for some time as the flames licked the blackened brick of the fireplace. It was almost like being home.

We were invited to stay the night that evening after being cooked a filling lunch and dinner. The generosity this family had shown us gave us a great appreciation for the Belgians as a whole. In training we were told we would be conquerors, liberating these people from the cruelty of the Germans. I had heard stories of the kindness our men had been shown as they fought their way across Europe toward Germany, but to experience it firsthand made all those stories seem like poor second-hand retellings. This family showed what I interpreted as appreciation in such a gracious and wholesome way that it almost produced tears. For the first time in a long time we were treated with tenderness. There were no men shouting orders, the cracking of gunfire, or death here. Though the army *had* taken care of us, this family—particularly the mother— took care of us in a different way. She brought us bowls of warm water to clean our dirty faces. She washed our clothes and fed us—unlike the army—things that were actually pleasant to eat.

Lunch was a dish of sliced fruit with more cheese. Dinner consisted of fried potato wedges and cubed meat with a savory gravy. This place was a paradise compared to what we had been through this far, and there were times, however briefly they came, where I forgot there was even a war going on at all just outside these walls.

Dieter and I slept in the living area by the fire. I let Dieter sleep on the couch and I slept on the floor. We were given pillows and blankets and even a glass of milk each before lying down for the night. I didn't want to sleep because I wanted to enjoy this moment, and the events of the entire day, for as long as I could, but sleep soon found me and sucked me into its black, all-encompassing void.

Nine

One would rarely dream during war. Nightmares were even rarer to come by. There were no circumstances the subconscious mind could conceive of that were worse than the current predicaments we soldiers found ourselves in. In war, sleep acted as a deep, black nothingness that took us from those scarred battlefields and frozen fox holes. That's not to say that sleep really *took* us anywhere, but simply made everything go away for a brief moment of time.

There was truly no nightmare greater than awakening to find you were still in the cold clutches of combat. To realize you were still frozen to the core and that some small, inconceivable scratch or nick had become ripe with infection. To awaken to find out another man you had known, however briefly, had been killed and left to rot where he fell.

To be a soldier during war—though calling myself one given my time in, and subsequent abandonment of, was surely considered treasonous—was hell in every hyperbolic sense of the word.

I awoke with a start to what I would learn was merely the clatter of silverware being placed on a long oval ceramic dish. Seeing my panic, the mother blushed and made an "I'm sorry to wake you" gesture. Though neither of us spoke the other's language, it was amazing how much information we could gather from the nod of a head or the wave of a hand.

Dieter and I folded up our bedding and returned it to the mother, who took it to the room we had changed in the day prior. When she returned, she had our uniforms, clean and neat in a woven basket.

Breakfast was waiting for us on the table: bread and cheese, and it was as delicious as it had been yesterday. This time however, we ate in an orderly and proper fashion.

After we had eaten, we returned to the living area where another fire had been lit, and though we vehemently despised the idea, we knew we could not in good conscience accept any more of this family's good graces. We knew it was time to move on.

We went into the back room and changed back into our uniforms. Though they were freshly cleaned, they paled in comparison to the heavenly, soft clothing we had been given. Our uniforms seemed stiff and uncomfortable, but they were familiar to our thin bodies.

The both of us then walked over to the door and the faces of the family who had selflessly taken us in looked both confused and sad. I clasped my hands together and bowed, not knowing how else to show my gratitude, and the mother rushed to the table and wrapped what was left of our breakfast in a cloth and gave it to me. I accepted her offering with a smile and to my surprise she hugged me. Her body felt so thin within my arms. Not from a lack of food, but simply the thinness of the female figure. I hadn't felt the touch of a woman before, besides my mother and sisters, and this gesture filled me with a comfort I had never really experienced. She stood straight and kissed me on the cheek, then moved to Dieter and did the same. My face felt red hot and I knew I was blushing.

The father rose from the couch in the living area and came over to shake our hands. His grip was firm and he looked me right in the eye. I found it somewhat hard to meet his gaze, but I held my eyes firm on his.

Then the boy came over to us, and mimicking his father, extended his hand, as well. It felt so small within mine, so tender and gentle. He had his father's eyes.

Once this was all over, I bowed once more before exiting their lovely little home. I wanted to look back as we walked away through the snow but I did not in spite of myself.

We carried on through the village and admired its wintery charm. Smoke rose from chimneys that stood proudly on snow-covered roofs. There were no light fixtures on the road, no stores or community buildings. Just a handful of wooden houses that sprouted up in the vast

Belgian countryside. Back home we call places like this a
one-road town.

Walking from one side of the village to the other took
maybe five minutes in total. Once through it was nothing
but snowy fields. Down the way you could see a wall of
trees, perhaps the same woods we had emerged from
that had looped back around in a U shape, half bordering
the village. Seeing them now, the strange fondness I had
acquired for those trees had gone, and I felt only dread in
seeing them again.

After another ten minutes of walking, my feet were
already wet. I wriggled my toes in my boots and felt my
socks squish under them like a loaded sponge. The reality
of our situation was abruptly showing itself again and the
memory of the dream-like reprieve we had experienced
was already fading.

I'm not entirely sure when I realized the dull droning
in my ears was that of a plane. Looking to the clear sky I
could not see anything, but as if in response to my searching eyes, an aircraft emerged from the top of the tree line.
There was no mistaking it, it was an American bomber.

When I snapped to look at Dieter, he was already
running for the trees, and without thinking I bolted after
him. Dieter had begun to veer to the right as to get out
from under the bomber's path. Given different circumstances, I may have been relieved to see such a wonder of
American engineering shoot across the sky like a spear,
but in this moment of fear stirred up by Dieter's immediate reaction I felt like prey scurrying for my life.

Once we hit the tree line we stopped to turn around, now clear of what that bomber carried in its belly, and as we spun, the bomber let go of its devastating cargo.

We watched in helpless horror as the plane blanketed that charming little village in a barrage of immense destruction. The explosions caused the earth to shake beneath us and snow fell from the drooping limbs of the pine trees. You could see the concussion of the blasts ripple across the snowy field toward us like a stone thrown into a pond, violently throwing the top layer of snow into the air.

I could not believe my eyes. In a matter of seconds the little village was completely decimated, along with all its inhabitants.

I don't know if I had ever felt such a deep hollowing of the soul in my entire life. It was clear there were no survivors. *What God damned strategic purpose did bombing that village serve?* I thought. The plane kept on and with hearts filled with sorrow and utter horror, we did too.

I had never felt so much hate toward this damned war than I had in the days that followed. It was a beast that perverted and destroyed everything it touched. How could humans do such things to each other? Why had so much innocence been caught in the middle? How could such horrible things happen to good people? God, where are you now?

After two more days of walking through the all-too-familiar woods, pausing every now and then to warm ourselves by the fire and returning to building primitive structures for shelter, I stopped and sat down in the snow. Dieter, noticing I was no longer following, also stopped and turned to me.

"Come on," he said, sounding equally as exhausted as I.

"I'm done," I replied in a heap on the ground.

Dieter walked over to me. "Come on, get up." He began reaching for my arms to pull me up.

I managed to slip from his grasp and pushed him away. He didn't resist and lumbered backward, regaining his posture lazily.

"So, what? You're just going to sit here?" he asked, huffing, with his arms slack at his sides and his back hunched over.

I didn't respond, keeping my eyes to the ground.

He began to walk away before turning sharply and marching back toward me in long strides. He reached for my arm again and I hit him. Not hard, more of a smack to the side of the head with the heel of my hand then a punch. He looked at me stunned, and before I had a chance to say anything, he threw his body at me, plowing me flat.

I don't know if I would call it a fight at first; it was more like the skirmish of flailing arms you see between two heated brothers. Nothing more than grunts escaped our mouths as we tussled in the snow. Then I punched him in the cheek, and he retorted with a jab to the nose. My eyes filled with tears and I grabbed his arm and bit down hard. Dieter shrieked and struck me with another blow to the face. Somehow I found what little strength I had left in me and managed to flip him onto his back and I swiftly mounted him. I began striking him in the face but his superior physical strength, even as spent as we were, prevailed once again. He flipped me back around and climbed on top of me. This time, instead of a hail of blows, he pulled the red nine he had holstered on his hip and held the barrel to my face. I let my arms fall to my sides outward and presented myself for him to shoot me.

"Go ahead, do it," I mumbled with blood running down my face from my nose and pooling in the back of my throat.

Dieter tensed down on the weapon and brought it closer to my face. We stayed locked like that for a charged moment before Dieter burst into a fit of coughing that shot spit onto my face and curled away from me like a dying insect, sliding off my chest. He flopped down beside me in the snow and began gagging in between violent, hacking fits that sounded thick with phlegm. I looked on, almost stupefied.

It took him some time, but after he had regained his composure and gotten his breathing under control—though a raspy rattle still emanated from his throat with every wheezing breath—we lay there staring up into the sky, completely drained from all of our physical exertion, I spoke softly, almost in a whisper. "We can go now."

"OK."

Ten

I did not have the energy to grieve. Being back in the elements once again took priority. There would be time for that later. There was a looming sorrow that hung over us both. We had eaten the bread and cheese we had been given, but kept the cloth they had been wrapped in for obvious sentimental reasons.

Dieter and I spoke little; perhaps we both felt embarrassed about our exchange and were waiting for the other to mention it. No apologies were needed; we had done so effectively by not killing each other.

He was clearly sick—with what, I did not know, but I wasn't going to bring it up until I felt I had to. We stopped for fires more frequently and stayed by them a little longer than usual. But he was a tough son of a bitch, that was the German in him, or maybe it was stubbornness that kept him going despite himself. More than likely it was a mixture of both.

Though the weather had warmed up some, it was still below freezing, but the sun was nice on the face. It made it so the top layer of snow would begin to melt, then refreeze in the night making it hard and a lot easier to traverse.

As we walked—the snow crunching under our feet—I decided to break this long silence between us.

"What did you do as a kid?" I asked. "You know, for fun."

Dieter had his arms wrapped around his chest. "My father was a—I don't know how you say—a shoe repairman."

"A cobbler?"

"Ah, yes. A cobbler. Funny word."

"How is *that* a funny word? All your German words sound funny to me. *Luffenwafer, donkeysure.*"

Dieter grimaced at my poor German pronunciations.

"OK, so, your dad was a cobbler . . ." I trailed off, giving Dieter a spot to carry on where he'd left off.

"Yes, from very young I helped him in his workshop. I would cut and stitch leather, I glued the soles of shoes back on. That sort of thing."

"This is what you did for fun?" I asked.

"It was very fulfilling."

Though interesting, this wasn't what I was after.

"There must have been other things you did for fun. That just sounds like work to me. You didn't ride bikes or anything?"

"Bikes? No. I did not have time for such things."

"OK, tell me about cobbling then."

"It was wonderful work. My father was a medic during the Great War. That's where he learned how to sew from servicing wounds. Trench-foot was a big problem in those times and he strived to fix and improve the men's boots to combat this. I guess he grew an admiration for footwear, because in the years following the war, he opened up his own shop. I learned a lot very young."

I thought back to when Dieter had so hurriedly had me remove my boots and started a fire to help me with my own feet. I remembered the efficient manner with which he'd proceeded. I guess it all made sense now.

Seeing as he didn't seem to have much of a playful childhood, or at least didn't care to share it, I pivoted the conversation.

"So was that your plan then?" I asked. "To take over the family business?"

"Someday, perhaps. I would be honored if he decided to give the business to me."

Man, I thought. *This kid isn't even twenty and it sounds like he has his whole life—at least in terms of a career— already laid out in front of him.*

"But that is a long way away," Dieter continued. "My father loves his work. He'll work till he dies."

"A proud generation," I stated, thinking of my own father, who also fought in the Great War, and also worked harder than anyone I had ever met. "My old man is a farmer back in Pennsylvania," I said.

Not understanding my meaning, Dieter asked me how old he was.

"*Old man* is just another term for *father,*" I told him. "He also fought in the war."

"Like us, our fathers were enemies."

This word had seemingly lost all meaning to me now.

"I guess they were," I replied.

Now Dieter carried on the conversation. "So, you are a farmer?" he asked.

"I am. I left school when I was fourteen to help manage the family farm. Hard work."

"Any siblings?"

"Three, all girls. You?"

"Just one brother."

"Is that how you learned to fight?"

"Oh, me and my brother fought lots." This brought a smile to his face, followed by a brief fit of coughing. "He was three years older than me, and he knew all the cheap tricks."

We shared a laugh, though his use of the past tense when discussing his brother filled me with a dull feeling and I decided not to ask what may have happened to him.

"Yeah, like what?" I asked, trying to ride the enthusiasm Dieter seemed to express while reminiscing about his brother.

"Oh, he was a real bastard. He would yank on my ears, stomp on my toes, and he always knew where to punch you to cause you to ache there for days."

"I knew a guy like that once," I said, thinking of Eugene.

"Absolute bastards, aren't they?"

"They absolutely are," I responded with a grin.

After that, we couldn't *stop* talking. We shared countless stories of youth and experience. There was lots of laughing and I found having my mouth curl into such joyful shapes felt as strange on my face as the prickly beard I now had.

Dieter had such an elegant way of telling stories. He spoke like a poet when recounting fond memories. He had a way of making simple recollections sound almost romantic in a sense. It was like he was reading aloud some kind of whimsical fairy tale from a far-off land that some writer would have loved to jot down for publication, though he was merely speaking about his childhood. I could have listened to him tell stories for hours, and for the rest of the day that is what I did.

That old familiar sound of combat began to creep its way through the trees again as the sun started its descent into the earth. We were definitely getting close to something, but could it really be coming from the same battle I had fled? Surely it was over by now.

Dieter had in fact been leading us back toward that area in search of his American sweetheart. We had made a wide berth around where I thought my regiment had been dug in near Foy, but in the pines, it all looked the same.

We ventured south, following a lonesome road cutting through the woods we had come across to distance ourselves from the sounds of gunfire and heavy artillery. Now that the sky had cleared, it was easier to determine our direction by the sun.

We figured we were back behind American lines as throughout the following day, American tanks could be seen roaring down the road we trailed alongside, accompanied by long lines of soldiers. When seeing these marching caravans we would retreat back into the woods and lay low until they passed. Though both Dieter and I wore American uniforms, and I had on my salvaged captain's long coat, my previous plan of assuming that role if confronted was thrown out the window as soon as those regiments came into view.

Our strategy of following the road soon proved fruitful. We began to come across battle-scarred towns where the buildings were made of brick and stone as opposed to the homes of timber we had seen thus far. Most buildings lay in ruin with debris and rubble scattered throughout the streets along with the dead.

Carefully we would scout the immediate area before bursting from the tree line to occupy a home for the night. We decided against fires as to not draw any attention from troops we knew to be somewhere in the area and instead wrapped our bodies in anything that would cover us. We did this for several days, slinking from one town to the next, surprised not to see much activity.

To Dieter, it seemed we were getting closer to wherever it was he intended to reach, though the completely devastated state we continuously found these once quaint and respectable little towns in visibly troubled him.

His health also began to worsen. He was constantly shaking, even when heavily bundled up in blankets. He wheezed with every breath and a clear liquid ran from his nose all throughout the day, which he wiped with the sleeve of his uniform until his nose had been rubbed raw.

Our pace had progressively gotten slower as he needed more time to stop and catch his breath between towns.

I did not protest these breaks, instead choosing to wrap him in the scavenged blankets I had slung around my own body. Through all this though, he remained in good spirits, and determined to keep moving.

In the fourth town we resided in, I had to convince him to stay another night despite his eagerness to press on. In that home, where we ended up staying for three full days and nights, he fell into a sleep from which I could not awake him.

"Hey, wake up. I got you some water."

Nothing.

"Hey, shoe shiner, let's go. You need to drink something."

Again, no response.

I knelt down beside him on the couch he occupied and shook his shoulder lazily. A sharp shard of anxiety fractured inside my stomach. Dieter's face was soaking wet as I rolled him over onto his back, and only from the dull wheeze coming from his throat did I know he wasn't dead. Regardless, I couldn't help but panic.

"Come on, bud. Wake up." I shook him more vigorously. Just beneath the thin skin of his eyelids, I could see the dull bulge of his irises moving back and forth.

A great loneliness struck me like a barrage of shrapnel from head to toe. I lumbered backward away from him at a complete loss for what to do. For a moment, I felt my worry was rooted in selfishness. If he was dying then I would be on my own again in this cruel landscape of cold and war. Was that a justified and reasonable response? Did guilt have a place here? Then I tucked those thoughts away into a dark corner of my mind.

Help him. That's what I needed to do right now. He would need medication, presumably Penicillin—*that* was what I needed to find.

I trotted all throughout the house, rummaging through cupboards and cabinets without success, these homes had already been looted. From an upstairs window I scanned the street below for any signs of life to only find death gazing back at me. The street was littered with the sprawling corpses of soldiers, soldiers I figured may still be brandishing personal medkits on their belts. It was the only option that presented itself.

Back at the bottom of the stairs I peered from the windows like a thief in the night and plotted my course. Just outside the front door lay three dead German soldiers. I would pilfer their medkits from their bodies and return back to the house to take inventory of their contents. If they did not contain what I needed, I would repeat the process, moving farther from the house as needed to reach the remaining fallen men.

Three. . . .

Two. . . .

One.

I launched from the doorway in a scuttle with my back level to the horizon. Coming up to the first man, who was face down in the street, I slid through the snow like a baseball player stealing a base and grabbed him by the shoulders. I spun him over and was presented with a ghastly sight. His mouth had been slit open from the fold of his lip to the ear on each side of his face emulating a haunting grin. It was a sight of pure horror, but as usual with such things, the eye does not want to look away. Due to these hanging flaps of skin, the entirety of the inside of his mouth was visible. Peering closer, unable to deter my eyes from doing so, I could see some of his teeth were gone. This wasn't the doing of a blunt object to the mouth or flying debris from an explosion, this was the not-so-graceful work of a knife.

I had heard stories of men removing the fingers from the corpses of the enemy to retrieve rings to take home as souvenirs or to simply sell off for booze or a box of crackers. I had also heard of men who fancied the collection of teeth that were capped in gold. By the looks of this man's gums that surrounded the empty gaps where teeth surely resided—gouged and sliced up—I figured that was what I was seeing.

When I was finally able to pull my eyes away, I went to work searching through the pouches that were fixed to this man's belt. The pouches were made from dark leather and were mostly uniform in appearance. There were six in total, with three on each side of the midsection above the hip. After the second pouch on the left side, I found what I was looking for.

It was a small, rectangular tin adorned with words I did not understand, but opening it revealed an assortment of vials, syringes, tools, and bandages. Satisfied, I snapped closed the tin and shoved it into the pocket of my captain's uniform and moved onto the next body.

Now knowing what I was looking for and where to find it, the process of looting was much quicker on the other two Germans. These men, however, had all of their teeth.

Accomplished in my goal of searching these three specific men, I darted back for the house to examine my findings.

On the wet plank floor just on the other side of the door, I lay everything out and discovered I could not understand what any of the labels said. What was the German word for *Penicillin?*

Damn it! This won't work. I'd need to find British or American soldiers on my next pass.

This town was undoubtedly the biggest of the three prior we had taken refuge in. There was a main street and several branching side roads that were lined with brick houses. It was so large, in fact, that it was easy to get lost in, so I developed a system of aligning bodies in such a way to find my way back to the house Dieter and I occupied. It wasn't elegant, but it worked.

After roughly an hour and a half of looting corpses, I still hadn't found what I was looking for.

The snow had begun to melt and sludgy sheets of watery muck were cast with every footstep. This did not help the condition of my sore feet.

Then from the corner of my eye, I caught a flash of movement down the street. I retreated to the side of a building to watch from the cover of a short concrete set of stairs. At the far end of the street was a man in civilian dress doing the very same thing I had been doing all morning. His hair was thin and stringy and hung wet from his head. He had a firm build but I could not make out many more details from this distance.

Hunched over a fallen American troop like some kind of cave troll, this man was rifling through the contents of his uniform. By now I was familiar with what a German, British, and American medkit looked like, and this man had the American soldier's medkit in hand and slid it into the pocket of his torn trousers. It appeared this man had the same intentions I did, and as he moved on out of sight down an adjacent road, I followed in pursuit.

I watched as he continued to plunder the fallen soldiers as he made his way down the road. Soon, his pockets were swollen with loot and he retreated around the back of a crooked building made of brick. Crossing the street after him, I heard the slam of a door and concluded he had entered the building through a cellar door in the ground. Seeing the wooden hatch-like door completely free of snow all but confirmed my suspicion.

Now I was presented with a choice: back off and continue my search for more medical supplies, which were surely within the pockets of this opportunistic civilian, or advance on this man's dwelling. Regardless of my urgency, I hesitated. Negotiation would be almost impossible due to the language barrier. Intimidation seemed the most viable option, though I questioned if I had the energy to pursue that path. The only other choice would be to simply burst in and kill him, and this was something I had no desire to do. After some thought, I determined my strategy.

I approached that cellar door and retrieved my pistol from its holster. With the joint of my thumb I clicked the safety down. I took some deep breaths and tried to mentally prepare myself for what I was about to do.

Reaching down, I wrapped my fingers around the door's handle and swung it toward me.

Eleven

I heaved the door open and it swung on its hinges, slamming into the ground beside me with an earthy thud. I rushed down the steep wooden staircase with my pistol drawn in front of me. The first thing that hit me was the smell. It was a rancid smell of excrement and infection. A smell that caused the eyes to water and the body to attempt to evacuate whatever little the stomach contained. The second thing I noticed were the hung lanterns, casting a warm, flickering glow that splashed onto the floor beneath them like streetlights. The third thing that became apparent almost instantly was the rows of cots, full of wounded men.

The man I had followed through the streets stood stiffly at the far end of the room with his hands in the air.

There was some mumbling from the men in their cots, but it seemed all were in too rough a shape to do anything more.

This was a makeshift aid station harboring soldiers from all nationalities. To my immediate left were two Americans, to my right, Germans. Beyond them were British with some civilians in the mix, as well. There must have been at least twenty-five wounded in this dank cellar.

As what I was seeing sank into my head, I thumbed the safety back on and lowered my pistol. Sliding it back into my holster, I held my hands—palms out—toward the rigid man who seemingly ran this operation, his pockets still stuffed with loot.

"Friendly," I said, trying to assert to him that I meant no harm.

"American?" he responded, to my surprise.

"Yes."

"Are you hurt?" asked the man. Though he had lowered his hands, there was some suspicion in his questioning. Our eyes were locked.

"No," I replied. "I have a friend who is very sick."

"With what?"

"I'm not sure. Pneumonia, perhaps."

"Where is he?"

"He's close by."

"Can you get him here?" asked the man.

"I couldn't wake him, but I think I can move him."

"If you can get him here, I will treat him the best I can."

I felt every muscle in my body relax as he said that, and he too seemed to experience something similar.

"OK," I said.

As I turned to leave with the eyes of a few of the wounded men following me, the man spoke again.

"What's your name, soldier?"

"Briggs, sir." Why I addressed him as *sir,* I do not know.

"No need for *sirs* around here, son." He spoke with a fatherly tone with only a faint accent I couldn't determine. "Go on and get that friend of yours, Briggs. I'll do what I can for him."

I responded with a sharp nod and hurried out of the cellar, closing the door behind me.

I crept through the sludgy streets back to where Dieter resided with the aid of the crudely positioned trail of bodies I had laid in the streets. Some looked back at me as I passed them with dry, foggy eyes and mouths agape, others merely looked to be asleep with doll-like complexions.

Reaching the building, I slipped inside to find Dieter right where I'd left him, his face still slick with sweat.

I nudged him with the faint hope he would awaken but it was clear he was still trapped within his illness, unresponsive. Regardless, I spoke to him as if we were speaking casually.

"Good news, buddy," I said rhetorically. "I think I might have found someone who can help. All I got to do is get you there." And it wasn't until I said this out loud that I realized the magnitude of this task. I was physically famished in all senses of the word. Putting this thought aside momentarily, I began to try and retrieve Dieter from the couch. I hooked my arms under his in almost a hugging gesture and tried to haul him up, but within seconds it became apparent I simply did not have the strength.

"Come on, you stubborn Kraut bastard!" I barked under my breath as I tried again with the same result. I lay Dieter's limp body back on the couch and took a moment to catch my breath. Even such a small burst of exertion had me completely spent.

I flopped down to the floor with a sudden dizziness and rested my back against the couch.

"You're not going to make this easy for me, are you?"

Once I had composed myself I began looking around the home for anything I could use that would assist me in moving Dieter. Nothing immediately presented itself.

"I need some sort of plank," I mumbled to myself and went to the window.

I scanned the rubble outside before coming to a door lying flat amongst the remnants of the building across the street.

"That might work," I said, and hopped into action without further thought.

I slid back out from the house and examined the road up and down for movement. Finding none, off I went.

The door was half buried in a mound of brick, timber, and wet snow. I climbed the mound and fastened my hands on either side of the door width wise. I gave it a modest pull but it seemed caught on something. Falling to my knees—as I did not have the energy to excavate this hunk of wood standing up—I began pushing bricks to the side lazily. Once the bricks were removed the problem became apparent. What was once most likely a supporting beam had the door pinched in place. I tried to lift it just enough to wedge the door out from under it, but its mass was too great. I simply sat back on my heels in defeat. I needed something to pry this hefty beam up, and I began searching the area. Luckily, the ground was littered with 2x4s that had been used as framing for the walls. I jammed a broken 2x4 about four feet in length into the small gap between the beam and the brick below. Then I gathered more bricks, and placed them under the 2x4, creating a seesaw type arrangement for leverage. Standing atop the length of 2x4 that pointed toward the sky, I began to bounce up and down, using my body weight to try and dislodge the beam. Promisingly, it budged ever so slightly. Again, I began to bounce, and the gap between the beam and the door widened. Seeing this, I shoved bits of crumbled brick in the gap. I repeated this process until I felt I had made enough room to retrieve the door.

Then I hopped from the 2x4 and went back to the exposed end of the door. The first pull shifted it slightly. The second pull dislodged it even more. In a one final yank, giving it everything my emaciated muscles could muster, the door slid out from under the beam. The sudden relief of the door from its imprisonment caused me to topple backward onto my rear end. The lumpy and jagged bed of brick caused me a great deal of pain. This entire endeavor was a true pain in my ass.

Sliding the door across the road, I felt like the ants I used to observe as a kid on the farm that would carry large cuts of leaves and grass back to their underground tunnels. It was a fitting comparison to my existence in the grand scale of war.

I lay the door just outside as I went to retrieve Dieter. Again I looped my arms under his and dragged his upper body across the room while his feet dragged along the floor. I pulled him through the entryway of our decrepit domicile and plopped him down on the door and took another moment to catch my breath. Surprisingly, I had worked up a sweat during all this labor and had to remove my captain's coat to cool off.

With Dieter on the door, I lifted one end and began to haul him down the street.

For the first time, I felt the snow-covered ground may actually prove to be a benefit. The door slid with ease through the sludgy muck and I thought that If I had had some rope, I could have pulled the door along like a sleigh to a much greater effect.

Regardless of this afterthought, we managed through the streets with a relative ease, only stopping every now and then to briefly rest my arms, which burned with fatigue. The entire trek took all but twenty minutes.

When I arrived at the crooked building that stood above the cellar, I was spent. My body trembled with exhaustion.

I hauled the door that harbored my friend around back and knocked on the cellar door. I was greeted by the man with the long thinning hair and fatherly tone and he helped me carry Dieter inside.

Again I was struck by the smell and wondered how anyone could remain down here for any length of time, but perhaps, like the war itself, you just got used to it.

We carried Dieter down the narrow but long cellar. Again, men who were conscious in their cots eyeballed us the whole way down.

Three empty cots lay unoccupied near the far end of the cellar and we carefully rested Dieter on one of them.

"How long has he been like this?" Asked the man.

"How long has he been sick, or unconscious?" I replied.

"Unconscious," the man retorted in short.

"It was just this morning that I couldn't wake him."

"OK," replied the man. "What were his symptoms before today?"

"He was coughing a lot. He had a wheeze, and would tire quickly."

"Any vomiting or diarrhea?"

"Not that I'm aware of."

"OK." The man rested the back of his hand on Dieter's forehead. "Unfortunately there is not a lot I can do besides give him some antibiotics and play it by ear."

I nodded in response. I knew there wouldn't be some magical cure that would cure his ailment immediately, but hearing him say this worried me a little.

"And if that doesn't work?" I asked, sounding more panicked than I would have liked to.

"Then he will pass in the coming days."

This rocked me to my core, though I knew it was out of my hands. Seeing this, the man tried to comfort me.

"Considering the circumstances, it's a good way to go," he said, then turned to retrieve a tin medkit. He opened it, and removed a syringe and a small bottle filled with a clear liquid. He then plunged the syringe into the bottle and extracted its content and prepared the syringe with a few taps from the back of his middle finger. "Can you cut open his uniform, exposing his shoulder?" he asked me, nodding to a small tray beside me that contained many different metal utensils. Seeing a pair of long, thin scissors, I did as he asked.

The man took a small packet from his breast pocket and opened it with his teeth and produced a thin rag from within. He rubbed Dieter's exposed shoulder with it before sinking the full length of the syringe into his arm.

"I'd advise you to sit," said the man, tossing the syringe onto the tray beside me. "You yourself look like you've seen better days."

I simply obeyed him and sat down on the empty cot behind me feeling a rush of exhaustion come over me now that I had no immediate task to pursue.

"Sleep, if you can. You look like you need it."

I stretched out on the cot, bringing my legs up from the floor and stole one more worried glance at Dieter.

"Don't worry about him," said the man, again in that fatherly tone. "He's not going anywhere."

I'm not sure if I even heard him finish his sentence before sleep fully encapsulated me.

Twelve

My eyes opened gently in the soft glow of the lantern that now hung between my cot and Dieter's in the long, dim cellar. I swung my legs to the floor tenderly and ran my fingers across my undoubtedly lice-riddled scalp. Looking around, becoming refamiliarized with my surroundings, I became aware of something curious. The smell that had assaulted me upon my arrival was now gone. But had it truly dissipated or had it just become something else I had adapted to?

"Morning."

I turned in my cot to see the balding man who had administered the shot into Dieter's arm greet me with a kind look on his face. He looked to be a man of about fifty. Broad shoulders, girthy arms. Probably was an athlete of some kind when he was younger.

I began to speak but he cut me off short by saying: "Two days," as if reading my thoughts.

I must have expressed a peculiar expression because he followed that up with: "That's usually the first thing someone in your shoes asks when they come to."

I shifted my gaze to Dieter and again he spoke without any questioning.

"Still out," he said. "But he hasn't given up on us yet."

"How long have you been here?" I asked him, turning my head back in his direction.

"Here? My whole life. I've only had this little operation going, maybe, three weeks now." He rose from the bedside of a soldier he had been tending to and strolled over to me, wiping his hands with a stained cloth.

"Hammes," he said, offering me his hand. I shook it.

"It's nice to meet you."

"Likewise," he responded.

"You have Germans in here," I said, scanning the two rows of occupied cots that lined the concrete walls.

"Got a few Brits, as well. Is that a problem?" he replied.

"No, of course not. No. I've just never seen anything like this."

"It's quite something, isn't it?" He too looked around the room, though he did it in the way one might when showing off a new car to a friend they had bought with hard-earned money. "Under all your uniforms and fancy metals you bleed the same color." He held up the blood-smeared cloth he had used to wipe his hands to accentuate his point.

I did not know how to respond.

"How are your feet?" Hammes asked me, tossing the cloth over his right shoulder.

"They're OK."

"They black?"

"Yes."

"Get those shoes off then. Keeping your feet clean and dry is the best thing you can do for them now."

I did as he asked and untied my boots and slid them off with great discomfort.

Hammes didn't grimace as I expected he would at the sight of my shriveled and blackened toes; instead, he sighed and had a look of disappointment on his face.

"Looks like you might lose those," he said in a rather matter-of-fact tone. Like he had seen this all before.

A flutter of anxiety swirled in my stomach.

"I'm going to get you a bowl of warm water. You're going to clean those feet then keep them up. I'll get you a pair of socks, as well."

"Yes, thank you," I said, almost sheepishly, before Hammes turned to go and retrieve what he had said he would.

Again my eyes wandered across the cellar to all the other wounded men. Some were asleep, some looked back at me, indifferent.

Hammes brought me the bowl of warm water and the socks he had promised as well as a cloth and I washed my feet. The warm water would have been extremely pleasant if it didn't cause such pain in my frostbitten toes.

After my feet were as clean as I figured they would get, I dried them off and lay back down on my cot.

"Hey," I heard someone hiss from a few cots down to my right.

I turned my head to see an American soldier propped up on one shoulder, belly down, facing me.

"What happened at Bastogne?" The soldier asked. "Did we hold it?"

"I don't know," I responded with a slight shake of the head.

"Damn," he replied. "What company are you in?"

I didn't know if I should have replied, but after a brief pause, I did.

"Easy."

All of a sudden I could hear the groans of cots as other American soldiers in the cellar rose up on their elbows to look at me. Even Hammes turned to me with a look of surprise on his face.

My eyes bounced from one man to the other.

"You're from Easy?" one soldier said.

"Holy shit," said another.

One man even hobbled to his feet, stood straight as a plank, and saluted me. I returned the salute, though I felt embarrassed and wrong for doing so.

"Were you part of the group that took out those AA guns at Normandy?" the original man who had mentioned Bastogne asked me.

"No," I said, "I didn't join until after Normandy. I'm a replacement."

All the men who had perched themselves up to see me flopped back down in their cots in disappointment as I said this, scoffing and grumbling. All but the first man who had spoken to me.

"I'm a replacement, too. Fox Company, he said. "The name's Scotty Emms."

"Henry Briggs," I replied with a shy, almost child-ish nod.

"Where you from, Henry Briggs?"

"Pennsylvania," I replied.

"Oh, yeah? Whereabouts?"

"New Hope. Well, just outside of New Hope."

"No shit!" exclaimed Scotty in disbelief. "I'm from Lambertville, New Jersey. Just across the Delaware."

I looked at him, stunned. You could practically toss a stone across the river from New Hope and it would land on the steps of Lambertville City Hall.

"I have relatives in New Hope," said Scotty.

I shook my head with eyebrows raised high on my forehead. "Small world." I said, not knowing what else to say.

"You been there long?" asked Scotty.

"Born and raised. I grew up on a farm just outside of town."

"That figures, you don't strike me as a city boy."

I chuckled at this.

"So, like, chickens and cows and such?"

"Some pigs, too," I replied with a smirk.

"No shit, eh. I hear farm life is rough, with all them animals dying and getting sick and whatnot."

"It can be. Nothing compared to here though."

"Oh, I'll bet. Nasty place, this is." Scotty did a brief scan of the room. "Did it prepare you for this at all? You know, killing cows and all that?"

"I don't think anything can prepare you for what happens over here."

"Amen to that," said Scotty. "I was a butcher for a bit, you know?"

"Oh, yeah?"

"You bet. I've held pounds of chicken hearts in my hands. Cut hogs in half with a bandsaw from snout to asshole. Even though it all looks the same, it's different when you see it here. No such thing as a clean cut. Everything gets chewed up, you know?"

I did know. I knew exactly what he meant. When my father taught me to butcher a cow, it almost seemed surgical. It was messy as all hell but if you cut where and what you needed too, it all came out cleanly. There was nothing surgical about what happened to men here. The beast of war *chewed* on everything before spitting it back out.

"Well," I said, "what happened to you that brought you here?" I gestured with my hands, referring to the cellar we both found ourselves in.

"I got separated from my group and then went and got myself shot in the ass! Can you believe that? It's quite common, really. I've had three buddies from my company shot in the ass. Dunny got shot in the ass soon after Normandy when I joined the company. Crenell was shot in the ass just crossing the street down the way. And Porter shot *himself* in the ass somehow just before we got to Foy. Dumb bastard still refuses to tell us how it happened."

It was quite pleasant to listen to Scotty Emms talk. He still had some humor in him, whether it was intentional or not. There was a carefree, almost oblivious attitude in the way he spoke that deteriorated in most men after long enough in combat. But somehow he had retained that trait.

"Yup," continued Scotty, "bullet went in one cheek and out the other. Four holes from one bullet. Well, technically I got five down there now!"

I could not help but laugh as he said this. It was rare to have a man joke about a wound acquired in combat so openly without trying to cover the immense pain and embarrassment he felt.

"Hammes says my biggest concern now is infection. Gotta keep it clean. Makes taking a crap quite the endeavor."

Giggles broke out from the other soldiers in the cellar.

"I gotta spread my cheeks like a goddamn New York burlesque dancer to take a shit!"

Laugher erupted from all the American and British men like booming marching drums while the Germans looked skeptically on. It wasn't hard to get swept up in the rolling tide of howling amusement that reverberated off the walls. I laughed until my eyes brimmed with tears and my cheeks physically hurt. It might have been the only pain I experienced during the war that I welcomed openly.

The following days were mostly like this. If there were quiet moments of sorrow and reflection, which there were, they would quickly pass as a soldier would start up with another story that would bring the cherished laughter back again.

Every day Dieter was administered another shot of Penicillin, though his condition hadn't changed.

We fed on K-rations Hammes had foraged from the surrounding area. It wasn't a lot but it was enough to keep us going and our spirits high. Each day that passed my admiration for Hammes grew as he selflessly continued to put himself in harm's way by going out foraging to care for us. If anyone ever deserved a medal or some form of official recognition for courage and bravery during war times, it was him.

I got to know some of these men fairly well during my time in this dark and stuffy cellar. Even some of the men who seemingly loathed me for simply being a replacement became friendly after not too long.

One evening, with the patter of rain drumming against the cellar door, I overheard Hammes and Scotty Emms talking. I don't believe they were trying to keep any of what they were saying from anyone else as it seemed casual but also somewhat remorseful. What I overheard was this:

Hammes had spoken with an American medic who had arranged a pickup of all the American and British men and would arrive within a few days.

It looked as if our time in the war was over.

At first, hearing this news worried me. Dieter and I had actively been avoiding American troops with fears of prosecution for desertion. But after everything we had been through as well as the time spent *here*—being fed and looked after, enjoying the company of other enlisted men—I felt it was time to accept whatever punishment I

95

would be given. Quite simply, I had had enough running. I had had enough of the cold and the struggle for survival. The hunger and the pain. I figured a jail cell was better than going back out there into the frozen hell I had endured for so long. I think after all of it, I had made my peace.

It wasn't until later that night that Hammes shared the good news with all of us. We cheered and cried and sang songs and began counting the seconds until the convoy of American Jeeps would arrive to take us away.

Almost every man pulled Hammes aside to speak with him personally and to thank him for everything he had done for them. Never had I seen a more humble man. He shook each of their hands with such resolve and compassion that I hoped that one day I could live my life by his example. I vowed to never forget his face and to always remember that all hope in man was not lost because men like Hammes existed among them.

When the Jeeps arrived two days later, Hammes helped every man out of their cot and up the steep steps of the cellar. Five Jeeps arrived in total, each only occupied by a single driver to carry as many wounded as possible. In total there were seventeen men evacuated that day, including Dieter and me. With the help of one of the Jeeps' drivers, a medic, we carried Dieter out from the cellar and into the back of one of the awaiting vehicles.

One of the drivers said to Hammes that they should take the wounded Germans, as well, to be treated before going off to a POW camp somewhere in the States, but he refused, stating he would give them the same chance he gave us, and that he would make sure they would be looked after and sent home to their families when possible. Seeing as none of the drivers had any rank to refuse such a decision, they finished loading up the wounded and began to take off.

I regret not having had any final words with Hammes before we left, there was just too much going on, but I saluted that man as the Jeep carrying me, Dieter, and Scotty Emms pulled away through the debris-littered street. He simply nodded and returned to his cellar.

Thirteen

Both Scotty and I hung our heads out of the topless Jeep and took in huge lungfuls of fresh, crisp air. The rushing air was cold and it bit into our faces but it was a refreshing kind of cold, like plunging into a river on a hot day. It awakened the senses; it gave you energy, and it made you humble.

Though a knot had begun to form in my stomach—knowing the ramifications that awaited me—I could not help but enjoy myself as the vehicle bumped up and down on the uneven terrain of the countryside roads.

The snow was all but gone from the warming weather and rain. Small white mounds still resided here and there, but the total blanket that once covered everything had been broken up.

Maybe I could make it out there now, I thought before slapping the thought away like a fly. *No, this is what must be done.*

Dieter's head lolled from side to side as the vehicle drove on. I thought that maybe for a moment I saw his eyelids flutter, but dismissed it as just idle movement caused by the bustle of the Jeep.

"I knew I'd make it through this thing," said Scotty with that casual grin that suited his face so well. "I just had a feeling, you know?"

"I still can't believe it myself," I replied.

"Well, believe it, good buddy. Soon, me and you are gonna be racing across the Delaware in our skivvies!"

I smiled, knowing that would likely never happen.

"You might even have to introduce me to one of those sisters of yours, Henry. I'm sure one of them will take a fancyin' to me. How could they not, I'm a goddamn war hero!"

Scotty slapped me on the back as he produced this bumbling laughter that bounced his shoulders up and down.

"Yeah?" I replied. "I can't wait to see you tell them just where you got shot."

"There's no shame in getting shot in the ass, my friend. I'll show my battle scars to them gladly."

Suddenly, I felt a hand on my forearm. When I turned I saw Dieter trying to sit up in the back of the Jeep, behind me.

"Where are we?" he mumbled.

"Good morning, sunshine," said Scotty, leaning over. "We, sir, are going home."

Dieter's eyes lazily shifted from Scotty to me as if for clarification.

"You've been out a long time. You're very sick but we're on our way to get you some help. Lie back down."

Dieter continued to try and rise but he simply did not have the strength.

"Where are we going?" he asked, seemingly somewhere between awake and asleep.

"Don't you worry about that now," I said, not wanting to alarm him by saying that we were heading toward an American field hospital. "I did a lot to keep your stubborn ass alive so I'm going to expect a very big *thank you* when we get there."

"How long was I—" but before he could finish, our Jeep was peppered with bullets. The vehicle violently swerved to one side and then the other, trying to regain control on the muddy road we were driving on. Scotty was thrown over top of me from the forceful swerving, then I was tossed on top of him. Dieter was hurled from the back of the vehicle.

When the Jeep finally came to a stop, all you could hear was gunfire, and shouting, and cries of pain.

I grabbed Scotty by the shoulder to pull him down but his head flopped limply into my lap. I cradled his head in my hands and lifted his face toward my own. His face was contorting into every shade of pain imaginable but he was still alive.

"I'm hit," he squawked, and I held him down to protect him from any incoming fire.

The driver had already disembarked the vehicle and was firing his side arm from the cover of the front of the Jeep.

Stealing a glance out of the back of the vehicle toward where the shooting was coming from, I could see Dieter trying to get to his knees on the road. Beyond him, nestled in a ditch to the far side of the curving roadway, I could see the flashes of gunfire.

Unplanned or not, this was an ambush.

I unlatched the door behind me that was furthest away from the shooting and spilled out onto the mucky road, pulling Scotty with me. I then crawled on elbows and knees to the ditch on my side of the road and tumbled into it. Checking to see if it was clear, I went back and retrieved Scotty.

"Stay here," I told him and began down the ditch. I had to get to Dieter.

The ditch was deep enough that I could crouch, and doing so, I scurried along the embankment. Poking my head up, I could see I wasn't far from Dieter now.

I had foolishly left my rifle at Hammes' but I still had my 1911 on me. I retrieved it and checked my ammunition; the magazine revealed only one bullet. With the bullet that was already chambered from the last time I had fired it, that gave me two shots. I slid the magazine back into the pistol, holstered it, and began searching my pockets for more ammunition and came across something that felt completely unfamiliar. Pulling it from my pocket, I recognized it as the cloth that had wrapped the leftover bread and cheese from our last breakfast with the Belgian family that had taken Dieter and me in and treated us so graciously. I knew I had kept it for a reason but did not think for the purpose I now might intend to use it for.

I popped my head up again amidst the sound of gunfire and bullets slamming into the sides of the other four Jeep. Locking onto Dieter, I emerged from the ditch and scurried toward him in the mud. He was on his hands and knees seemingly in a stupor and unaware of what was going on all around him. I grabbed him by the arm and dragged him back to the ditch on his back.

Once safely in cover, he began fighting me weakly, unaware who had grabbed him.

"It's me! It's me," I barked and he calmed down at the sight of my face. "We gotta move. Can you move?"

Dieter shook his head and I wasted no time in again grabbing his arm and dragging him along the muddy ditch.

Soon we had regrouped with Scotty and I asked him if he had his side arm.

"It must have fallen out," he responded, still visibly stricken with pain. "They shot me in the fuckin' ass!" he shrieked. "In the goddamn ass!"

Then I remembered Dieter still had his red nine. I patted his body and found it in its holster. Taking it out, I checked the action to see no bullets in the weapons reservoir.

The whole time this thing had been empty.

I looked over to the Jeep Scotty and I had come from to see the driver struck and collapse to the ground. I could maybe go for his weapon but odds were his munitions would be spent, as well. Sinking back into the ditch beside Scotty and Dieter, I realized I had exhausted all of my options. I retrieved the cloth from my pocket and waited until the firing had ceased.

Everything that had occurred from our vehicle first being struck to this very moment may have only taken less than a minute.

Once the firing had stopped, I heard a German voice barking commands to his men. This is when I took the cloth in my hand and held it up over my head. There was no other choice but to surrender.

A shot rang off here, a shot rang off there, no doubt they were executing the men that were beyond any chance of survival. Had they all been killed? I was unsure.

"Stand up!" a voice beckoned, unmistakably German.

I did as commanded.

I rose with my trembling hands above my head still clutching the cloth. In front of me stood a German officer in a long, dark coat. Behind him stood six or seven men with rifles in hand, smoke still pouring from their barrels.

"Is it just you?" asked the German officer.

"There are two here with me," I replied, frozen stiff.

"Tell them to stand up!" he shouted at me.

"They are wounded, I don't believe they can stand."

The officer looked to his men and gave a swift nod in my direction. Two of his men came walking toward me with their weapons raised. The two men observed Scotty and Dieter and called back to their commander in German. The officer yelled something back to them and they began lifting both Dieter and Scotty up off the ground. Dieter was quiet and compliant but Scotty yelped and whined.

"Come," demanded the officer and I began toward him. Dieter walked with the aid of one man, but Scotty needed two of the German soldiers to carry him along.

I heard Dieter mumble something to the soldier who was aiding him. With a look of shock, the soldier relayed whatever Dieter had said to the officer. The officer let out a low chuckle and spoke directly to Dieter. Dieter replied and the officer turned to me, now standing ten feet away in the road.

"He tells me he is German," said the officer with a slanting face and low-hanging, oily eyelids. The two men who were aiding Scotty sat him down on their side of the road and he rolled over onto his belly in the mud.

"He must be mistaken," I said, wondering why he would have told them that. "He is very sick and must not be thinking clearly."

The officer spoke to Dieter again and Dieter replied, his eyes barely open.

"His German is very good," the officer assured me. "But you say he is not. Who do I believe?"

I straightened up, trying to reaffirm my prior statement with my posture. The officer turned to Dieter. "You say you are German; prove it."

The officer pulled his side arm from its holster and held it out to Dieter. It was in immaculate shape, it probably had never been fired. "If you are German, as you say, then kill this man." He gestured toward me.

Dieter's eyes widened at this as if awoken by some spoken spell. The officer then placed his side arm in Dieter's hands.

"Go on then, kill the enemy."

Dieter now looked more alive than I had ever seen him as he wrapped his hands around the pistol. His eyes blazed with a fire that frightened me beyond words. He raised the pistol with both hands, his arms staggering as if under tension from some invisible bands. His face became unreadable.

I stood there feebly with my arms at my side and my head slightly down, finding it hard to look in his direction. If this is what he needed to do to survive, then so be it. He would go back home and work for his father repairing shoes. He might even end up finding Patty in some twist of fate and settle down and have a family. He may or may not be eighteen now, I was unsure of the date. I was closer to thirty than I was to his age.

I meant it when I said I had found my peace. All my options had now expired and I found myself at the end of the road. At least this way, if his aim was true, it would be a quick death.

"Well, go on, you *cocksucker*. Do it." I demanded.

As if struck by some unseeable force, Dieter's face had changed. The wild look in his eyes began to crumble and decay into something vulnerable. I could see him beginning to cry. It wasn't an explosive reaction but a subtle one. Tears began to run down his gaunt face and drip from his chin like a leaky faucet. His lips trembled.

The gun in his hands was still pointed directly at me but it was then I knew he couldn't pull the trigger.

He dropped his arm in defeat as he deflated and stumbled backward, handing the pistol back to the officer. The officer ran his tongue over his top teeth with a look of indifference.

Every muscle in my body turned to liquid.

"Shame," said the officer. "I would have liked to see that weapon fired." He nodded to one of his men and the soldier raised his rifle and shot Dieter dead on the spot.

PART II:

A CLOTH OF ASHES

"War does not determine who is right, only who is left."
-Unknown

Fourteen

I was ushered at gunpoint to the side of the road where Scotty lay with the few others who had survived the assaults as we awaited transport vehicles to take us to God-knows-where. The once peaceful countryside road was now scattered with the bodies of the men I had been joking and laughing with the night before and the Jeeps we rode in sat at odd angles on flat tires with trails of bullet holes slinking from bumper to bumper. I could not take my eyes off Dieter's body as it lay, face down, in the mud.

He should have fired. Even if he got me in the arm or the leg it may have proved his allegiance to the German officer and he may have been spared, or maybe his fate had already been determined the minute he spoke in his native tongue and the officer just wanted a spectacle.

Death is such a peculiar thing. One minute the person is there, the next they are not, but the body remains. I can still see his hair being tossed around in the gentle breeze.

His hands looked no different. Aside from the blood that drained from the hole in the back of his head and pooled around his face on the ground, he looked as he had for the last week. He looked to be sleeping, only sleeping. As much as I tried to convince myself of this, I could not refute what my eyes had seen. A single shot and down he went as if removing the cord that powered an automaton.

As I sat there, I felt as if my innards had been scooped out and I was nothing more than flesh and bone. That between my neck and groin was just an empty cavern of negative air. I felt lost and utterly defeated.

I thought of charging the German officer who had orchestrated this fatal display in the hopes that I too would be cut down. I was now a German prisoner of war and that seemed like the most promising thing I could look forward to. But if they gunned me down then what stopped them from killing the rest who had survived who sat beside me in some primal blood lust?

To my left sat Scotty Emms, Ronald Greer, Oliver Whitmore, and two of the medic drivers, whose names I did not know.

The only *recently* injured among us was Scotty, with a wound to the rear end. Ronald had been recovering from a leg wound on his upper thigh and Oliver had a bandage wrapped around his head, covering one eye. The drivers were unharmed.

It began to rain as we waited and the officer made those of us who could, walk. I, Oliver, and the two medic drivers pushed the Jeeps off the road. The condition of the mud only worsened in the moderate downpour, causing us to frequently lose our footing and fall to the ground as we pushed the vehicles. Once the road was cleared, we were called back. Behind me, one of the medics said, "We should move the bodies."

Most of those killed in the assault never made it out of the vehicles, but some had and now laid strewn across the road, Dieter among them.

The German officer swung around and glared at the medic who had spoken. It looked like he was about to say something cruel and unthinkable, but after chewing on the corner of his lip he gave us a nod.

I made sure I was the one who tended to Dieter and I hauled him up and over my shoulder. How I had the strength to do so was beyond me, but I managed with little struggle.

The ditch on the opposite side of the road was the only suitable place to lay these men. We had neither the time nor the tools to give them a proper burial.

I carried Dieter off to the ditch and rested him down gently and with care.

Sleeping, only sleeping.

"Until we meet again, my friend," I muttered to him, surprised by the catch in my throat as I said this. My eyes welled with tears but none fell down my face. I removed my captain's jacket and lay it over top of him, covering his face. I then took the cloth I had used to surrender that had been given to me by that wonderful woman, and placed it in his pants pocket.

The roar of an engine could be heard coming around the bend and I looked up to see the arrival of a light brown truck with a long, wood-paneled bed that had a canopy of black canvas. The German officer let out a sharp whistle and those of us who had moved the bodies from the road shuffled toward it. As I went, I took one last longing look at Dieter, who lay flat at the bottom of the grassy ditch, before lowering my head and moving along.

We were lined up in single file at the back of the truck before piling inside, one by one. Both Scotty and Ronald needed assistance climbing aboard, a task left to me and the medics. To our surprise, the back of the truck was already half-filled with civilians who wore filthy clothing and shocked expressions on their faces. They would look at us briefly before turning their heads away as if caught staring at a disfigured invalid.

We found empty spaces on the wooden benches that ran the length of the truck bed and quietly sat down, some of us shoulder to shoulder with the truck's occupants. None met our gaze or attempted to converse in any way.

I could hear the officer speaking with the truck's driver, followed by the sound of the doors clicking open, the truck's suspension dipping momentarily as I assumed the men got in, then the door slamming shut.

The entire time the vehicle's engine rumbled idly, but now with a monstrous roar it came alive and we began moving. All of us in the back bobbed from left to right, bumping into each other as the truck shifted gears while it gained speed. Once the acceleration subsided and the vehicle settled at its cruising speed, we continued to bounce around due to the uneven country road beneath us.

We rode along like that in grim silence for what must have been hours. Some among us became ill from the constant bobbing of the vehicle and vomited between their feet. Across from me sat a beautiful woman with a baby clutched to her breast. Beside her was a boy of about ten who shared a resemblance to the boy of the family who had accepted Dieter and me from the cold and treated us so tenderly.

He wasn't the only child in the back of the truck. There were others—some young, some older, all with the same wide-eyed look of terror on their smooth faces. Little did I know most of them would be dead by nightfall.

When we seemingly arrived at our destination, we were marched out of the truck and told to stand in line in front of a long white wall, where a row of German guards stood watch, accompanied by two other trucks similar to the one we had arrived in, off to their right.

As I stepped out of the back of the truck, I scanned the row of guards. They all stood straight with their chests protruding and chins held high. One, however, did not share this mechanical stance no matter how hard he seemingly tried to emulate it.

Immediately after we had been arranged in a line, the women and children were separated and ushered onto one of the awaiting trucks. There were some cries as the husbands and fathers of these women and children protested and they were beaten into order.

Then the remaining men, including me, were forced to remove their trousers and present their genitals to the guards. Those who were circumcised were escorted to the other truck, including Oliver. Those who were not remained in line.

The German officer who had ordered Dieter's death and ridden along with us to this place, rounded the vehicle we had arrived in and stood before us.

"If you do as you are told and work hard, you will live." He then repeated the rule in a few other languages.

Once satisfied, he motioned to the guards who lined the wall and they stepped forward and ushered us through a gate about four men wide. Above the gate were words in German I did not understand that had been formed in iron bars and above that stood a three-tiered rectangular brown building with a clock at its peak.

Inside was a large gravel courtyard, perhaps two or three football fields in width and two in length. Beyond that were rows and rows of long rectangular buildings that radiated outward like a slice of pie, though such imagery in a place like this seemed cruel to envision.

Our group of maybe twelve men and a few teenage boys were ordered in threes and taken to a pile of clothing that stood an unbelievable twenty or thirty feet high and ran for as far as the eye could see. It contained every article of clothing you could imagine. Beside this pile stood another impressively large mound of what looked like metal wiring or mechanical gauges, but upon closer viewing, proved to be a tangled mess of eyeglasses.

We were told to remove all of our clothing and toss it into the pile. Any valuables, such as rings or other jewelry, were collected by officers carrying tin boxes. Finally, those of us that still carried firearms or dog tags were told to surrender them to the officers.

From there we were shuffled, naked, to a simple-looking long building with arched halls where we were to bathe in tubs of murky ice cold water and chlorine. The smell of the chlorine was so strong my eyes watered and my nose and throat burned as I inhaled. We were then taken to have our heads and beards shaved by prisoners of the camp and were given striped uniforms that resembled pajamas and wooden clogs and numbers. Mine was 117031. These prisoners who were given these undesirable tasks worked with factory-line efficiency. Their faces were blank and emotionless, though not from a sense of superiority or callousness but more of a completely broken sense of humanity. As if to destroy our deteriorating mental well-being even further, a truck like the one we arrived in sat just outside the window of this building. It's canopy had been removed and the wooden sides hung from the truck bed like an open book. On the bed itself were dozens of skeletal corpses stacked on top of one another like firewood. It was almost indistinguishable to tell which thin, ropey limb belonged to which emaciated body. Most of what I saw didn't even appear to be human. *Those things out there couldn't possibly be human.*

Beyond that was a brown triangular building with a large chimney that spewed a dark, curling smoke.

Moving down the hall into another station, we were given shots in our arms by more inmates in white coats who bore the same expressions of those who had cut our hair. It seemed the Germans were taking every precaution not to physically touch us until we were sterilized and inoculated from whatever filth and disease they thought we carried.

A new group of German guards awaited us once we exited the building and filed out into the courtyard with our prickly new haircuts and thin striped uniforms, with leashes in their hands. At the ends of these leashes were lunging dogs that barked feverishly at us with teeth bared and lips curled back to the gum line.

"My men don't seem to like you," said one guard, referring to the dogs through an arrogant grin. "It's been awhile since they've seen Americans."

A few of the other guards laughed at this. I kept my head down.

These men and their dogs escorted us throughout the camp, barking and chomping at our ankles with foaming mouths, to our barracks: Block 40. How foolish I had been to believe it could not get any worse.

If I thought the smell of Hammes' cellar was bad; the smell that first greeted me as the door swung open to Block 40 made that place seem like a highly coveted spa for a femininely weekend retreat. The air was putrid and seemed to coat the lining of your mouth. *You could taste the smell.* In war I had smelled the damned, dead, and decaying, but this was beyond description. This is what cruelty smelled like.

The assault on my nose was then followed up by an assault on the eyes. The block was long and narrow, and running along either side were bunks stacked four high that went from floor to ceiling. These bunks looked to be made of raw framing timber painted brown and were barren of any mattresses or padding. Inside each bunk, which ran perpendicular from the walls, harbored three to four malnourished men.

Their angular, bird-like heads turned to face us as we entered into the block. Their eyes sunk into their faces like wells above their protruding cheekbones. Their skin looked as if it had been pulled tight and stretched across not only their skulls, but their entire bodies. Those who stood were barely clothed while others wore nothing at all. I once thought *I* looked thin after weeks with little food, but these men—who surely had to be reanimated corpses because their sheer existence defied all known reality— were horribly emaciated. They looked no different from the pile of bodies I had seen as I had my hair cut. But *those* bodies I figured had been dead for weeks—months, even—and had gotten that way from the dry, crisp air and withered in the sun. But before me were *living* men that shared their resemblance to a staggering degree. It was hard to even call what I was seeing *men.* No, these were poorly upholstered skeletons. *They had to be.* Nothing but skin and bones. How could anyone get like that and survive? I did not know.

I waddled inside with the others and found a bunk on the bottom level, practically flush with the floor, occupied by only two men. To my surprise, they shuffled over and presented me a place to fill. I crawled in and the others I had arrived with did the same, finding their own vacancies.

"Be ready in fifteen minutes," commanded one of the guards to all who were present. "We are going back to the graveyard."

Saying this, the guard slammed the door behind him and left. All was silent save the creaking of wood as the men of the bunks settled back into the positions they had been in prior to our arrival.

I looked around in a speechless stupor before my eyes aligned with those of Scotty Emms, who was across from me about seven bunks down. He shook his head, raised his eyebrows, and hung his mouth slightly agape as if to say, "I have no answers."

A low, gravelly bark came from beside me and I turned my head toward it.

In a thick accent I assumed to be Russian, a man with a leathery face said, "Sleep, if you can."

I heard what he said but my brain seemingly didn't register the words as having any known meaning. He may as well have spoken to me in Russian.

After a long pause I mumbled, "What is this place?"

Somberly—in the same tone a doctor might say, "The baby didn't survive" to a new mother, or more aptly, "You are looking at two, maybe three weeks left to live" to a man who the month before found a lump on his chest—he said, "This is Buchenwald, my poor boy. This is a very, very bad place."

Fifteen

There was no way I was getting any sleep in the fifteen minutes I had before the guards returned. I wasn't sure I would ever be able to sleep again after all I had seen of this nightmarish place.

It was then, once the creaking of bunks had subsided, that I realized I was crying. Perhaps it had just started or perhaps I had been crying since walking in through the gates of this *hell* I now knew to be called *Buchenwald*. But I could not control my convulsive sobbing and decided to give into it entirely. I don't believe I was just weeping for the current state I found myself in. I believe I was weeping for everything I hadn't had the chance to mourn properly until right then. The wife I had widowed in the cave, the family that took me in only to be eradicated by American carpet bombing, and Dieter, *my poor friend Dieter*.

I did not wail or bray, this was more of a quiet *implosion*. A complete breaking down due to the things I'd tucked away into the dark corners of my mind that now came rushing back into the light.

The man beside me in the bunk lay a comforting arm over my shoulder and held me as I wept, and as if by pure child-like instinct, I embraced him and we lay there together.

I was pulled out of my inconsolable state by a powerful jet of freezing cold water. A guard stood at the door of the block with a firehose in his hands and sprayed everyone in their bunks. Some shrieked and some moaned but all began to climb out and down from their beds in a zombie-like fashion.

"Come on," whispered the man who had been comforting me during my meltdown, and he helped me out of the bunk.

"You! *Ami!*" barked the guard, though I was unaware he was referring to me.

The man beside me gave me a gentle nudge and gestured to the guard with a nod of the head.

"Yes?" I said, trying to compose myself.

"Count the dead and report to me outside." He then said something in German and everyone in the block shuffled out through the door.

Once empty, I turned to see the tops of several shaven heads resting in the bunks. *They couldn't be dead, could they?"*

I walked down the center of the barracks and began counting all the heads I could see. Once I had a number,

I counted again before exiting the block and was met outside by the awaiting guard.

"Well?" he said, looking down at me over his straight nose.

"Twenty-four," I mumbled.

"Speak up!" he shouted.

"Twenty-four!"

"Good," said the guard, then positioned himself as if he expected something more from me.

After a brief and ominous pause, he spoke again.

"What are you waiting for?"

"I don't understand," I replied.

"Bring them to the truck. We won't wait forever."

With that, he marched over to the group that had been in Block 40 with me, who had gathered outside and were standing shivering, awaiting further instruction, and commanded them to run.

Horrified with the job I had been assigned, I turned and went back inside and began removing the dead from their bunks.

I don't know how long it took to drag each skeletal corpse from Block 40 to the truck that had been parked by the building where I'd had my hair cut. The task was grueling, exhausting, and disturbed me greatly. I had to dehumanize these men into something else to be able to get through it and keep what little sanity I was struggling to hold onto. My mind needed to be blank and to not think of the possible upbringings and histories of these people. I could not think of them as husbands and fathers and sons, but mere cargo that needed moving. That was all they could be. Though I tried, it was an impossible mental feat to accomplish.

When I was finished, I dragged my feet back to the guard who had assigned me this punishment and he called the group in from jogging around the barracks.

"I'm sure some of these men won't be too thrilled you made them run for so long," he said to me out of the corner of his mouth.

When the group had reassembled in front of him, panting and hunched over, he addressed them in German. As he spoke, some of the crooked men glared at me with sharp eyes and curled lips.

"Zu den lastwagen!" he barked, and the group filed out in a column of bony and jagged bodies. I followed in behind.

We were loaded into trucks and driven to a cemetery roughly thirty minutes from Buchenwald. Scotty, Ronald, and the medics were in another truck and no one would look me in the eye in the one I had been crammed into. The Russian, however—the man who held me in my moment of weakness—sat three men down, opposite from me and turned his head in my direction.

He was a man I believed to be in his sixties, though he could very well have been younger. Everyone here looked older than they probably were—that's what subhuman captivity does to a man.

He rose and sat beside me.

"What is your name, son?"

"Briggs, sir. Henry Briggs."

He smiled faintly. "Avenir Akinfeev, and there is no need for that kind of talk with me." We shook hands, a strange formality given these informal circumstances.

Once our hands parted, I scanned the faces of those around me.

"Don't worry about them, they aren't angry with you, they are tired. They know the games the guards play. They know who to direct their frustrations at," said Avenir.

"Where are we going?" I asked.

"To a resting place for my people."

"Russians?"

He chuckled at this as if we were joking with one another on a backyard patio over a cup of tea.

"Jews," he corrected. "We are going to a cemetery for Jews."

"Why would we be going to a cemetery for Jews?" I asked.

"For the gravestones." Avenir's face shifted into a more somber expression. "They have us destroy the gravestones of our people and use the rubble to build roads."

I felt the truck slowing down before coming to a full stop and men began to stand to exit the vehicle.

"Do what they ask of you and you will be fine," said Avenir as I followed him out into the sunlight.

Once outside, I regrouped with Scotty, Ronald, and the medics. They were hard to find given that maybe 100 men in total had disembarked from the trucks. Once I approached, Scotty placed a hand on my shoulder and said, "You seem to be in better shape than you were before. You all right?"

Somehow his charm had remained after all we both had seen.

"I'm fine," I said with a shallow nod. "You seem better, as well. How's your ass?"

"Ah!" he scoffed playfully. "It's not too bad. 'Tis but a flesh wound, as they say. I can show you if you want?"

This brought a smile to my face. "Another time, maybe. Ronald, how's the leg?"

"It's sore, but I can walk," he replied, shortly.

"Good," I said. "And you two," I addressed the medics, "I never got your names."

One of the medics stepped forward. "Tom Collins, like the drink. This is Barney Kershaw."

First Barney extended his hand, followed by Tom.

"The hell you think they got us out here for?" asked Ronald.

Beyond the group of men stood rows and rows of gravestones. It may have been the largest cemetery I had ever seen. Some headstones were small, flat squares of dark marble, others bore a more traditional look. But some looked to be monoliths standing fifteen feet high above the grass. Some were large pyramid-shaped blocks of white stone, some were adorned with statues of angels holding buckets or birds. Paved pathways ran throughout the cemetery like snakes and wooden benches were dotted along them.

"We're here to destroy the gravestones," I said in a low, subdued tone.

"Destroy the gravestones?" Scotty repeated. "What they got us doing that for?"

"Roads, I think. I'm not sure."

A German guard shot and killed a man simply to rally our attention. All of our heads snapped toward the direction of the shot before the body hit the ground.

Satisfied, the German began speaking. Once he had finished, he switched to English.

"Where are the Americans?" he shouted.

I raised my hand despite myself and he marched over.

"You are here to break these gravestones into pieces no bigger than a head." He pointed to the man he had shot on the ground. "There is your reference, if needed. The black truck will have the tools you need. I very much like those tools and if one is broken I will be very displeased, do you understand?"

All of us Americans nodded in agreement.

"That man there," he pointed back to the dead man on the ground, "broke the handle of a spade the last time he was here. I trust you will treat the tools better than him." He glared at us under his strong, lowered brow before walking off.

A whistle was blown and the large group that was huddled along the side of the road began to migrate to the truck with the tools.

In its bed were mostly pickaxes. There were a few shovels and heavy bars of about four feet. I grabbed a pickaxe when my turn to choose a tool became apparent and lumbered into the cemetery with it in my hands.

Upon walking onto the cemetery grounds, which no fences bordered, I could see that men had already been at these gravestones. Some had been broken down until barely any stone remained protruding from the grass; others had been dug out completely.

Picking a gravestone at random, I stopped in front of it momentarily to apologize to whomever lay below it. Everything about what I was expected to do felt wrong—not only in a moral way, but in a divine way, as well. I took one last breath of regret and swung my pickaxe.

We did this for twenty-four hours straight.

Many worked themselves sick, though their guttural heaves produced little if anything at all. If one was to collapse of exhaustion, a "working accident" would occur. In the first few hours of our being there, a "working accident" consisted of a fatal beating. The more time that passed, a simple gunshot achieved the same result.

There were five trucks in total in the convoy that brought us there. Three were for the men, one carried tools, and the other truck was for hauling the rubble produced from chipping away at the gravestones until they were gone. Of course, we weren't given wheelbarrows or anything of the like. Instead, we carried the crumbled stone by hand. Doing it this way was obviously less efficient, almost to the point where I wondered if there even was a road being built at all or if this was just another way to destroy the Jewish prisoners even more by desecrating a place that harbored their dead. Having to move such quantities of stone handful by handful only made their suffering worse.

When the final whistle blew for us to return to the trucks, I was completely spent. We had been given no food or water during our entire time picking at those gravestones and I felt I could collapse at any moment.

There were twelve "working accidents" by the time we were finished. Looking at the sprawling fields and gentle rolling hills of the cemetery as a whole, we had barely cleared even a small fraction of its grand scale. I tossed my pickaxe into the back of the truck and set out to find Scotty and the others to ride back with. They all looked equally as shot as I did.

We managed to climb into the back of the same truck, our hands raw and bleeding, our bodies filthy with dirt. We didn't even have the energy to mutter a single word to each other the whole drive back.

When we got back to Buchenwald, we were each given a ration of bread as we stepped out of the truck one by one, and were told the trough on the outside of our block had been filled with water.

I attempted to take a bite of the bread but my teeth weren't able to penetrate it and my total lack of energy made my following attempts also unsuccessful, regardless of how feverishly hungry I was. It was like trying to crumble gravestones with a blade of grass.

As we shuffled back to our block, limping with stiffness and twisted with cramps, a guard called for Tom and Barney, the two medics.

"You know how to administer injections, yes?" asked the guard.

Both men nodded.

The guard then pointed to another guard who was making his way toward us.

"Go with him," said the guard, and the two medics sheepishly obeyed.

We all took turns scooping handfuls of water from the trough and bringing them to our withered lips. The trough of water was swirling with grit that would crunch between your teeth and had what appeared to be oil on its surface, but this did not stop us from emptying that trough dry.

You would think men in conditions such as this would go after the water like a pack of feral dogs, but instead they were patient and seemingly cordial about it. They made sure every man had a drink before it was gone. I even saw one man lifting cupped hands of water up to the mouths of those who did not have the strength to do so themselves. There was a unity amongst these men, a kinship formed in the face of oppression the likes of which history had never witnessed. Seeing something like this moved you in ways that are impossible to describe. It both healed and fractured the soul.

Back in our bunks, Avenir produced a piece of sharp stone that he used to cut our pieces of bread. Once he'd cut his into manageable chunks, he offered me half his ration.

"Why would you give this to me?" I asked him in bewilderment.

"You remind me of my son," he said flatly. "Eat."

My eyes brimmed with admiration, and before I could finish eating all of my bread, sleep found its way to me and into the void I went.

Sixteen

This was our daily routine for the next two long weeks at Buchenwald. Awoken by hoses, crammed into trucks, driven to the cemetery, work, come back, eat our rations, sleep. It was miserable, and to say it was exhausting is to do so merely for lack of a more descriptive word. We turned into the walking dead performing our duties. Every morning we would discover that more had passed in the night and others had been brought in. One would be picked at random in the morning to remove the dead in their bunks like I had done my first day. It seemed like a never-ending revolving door from which we could not escape.

Avenir told me of the camp's history over several days. Particularly of the woman known as *the Bitch of Buchenwald.*

Isle Koch was her real name, and she and her husband ran the camp in its early years. This woman appeared to me as cruel beyond words.

She had a fascination with tattoos, Avenir told me, as we swung our pickaxes. More accurately, the tattoos of the prisoners. She devised experiments for these men, experiments that had no result in mind except for a painful death. She would then have the skin removed that contained the desired tattoos she admired and display them as art in her home. She used the tattooed skin as book covers and had lampshades made. Most of the decorated flesh was framed and hung on her walls or sat on coffee tables. It was even rumored that she used the fingers of the Jewish prisoners as light switches.

Her sadistic methods were also practiced in other ways. She would ride often around the camp on her beloved horse when her husband was away attending to other matters, dressed in clothing that revealed her voluptuous figure. She would pick out a group of men—primarily young men—who were to strip naked and then were forced to watch her as she rode. If these young men were to show the telltale signs of male arousal, they were tortured and killed.

She filled her mansion that resided on the camp with young handsome men as servants and would parade around in the nude. She used her sexuality as a lure the way the Venus fly trap secretes nectar to attract its prey before snapping shut, sealing the fate of any curious passerby.

As Avenir put it: "She was the devil disguised as a woman."

After we had completed the gargantuan task of clearing the Jewish cemetery of its gravestones, the men of Block 40 were reassigned to the camp's rock quarry, where they did more of the same grueling work. All but we Americans—myself, Scotty, and Ronald—were given a more grim and perverted task. We were to remove the remains from the camp's incinerators and crush them down into a fine powder, of course, by hand.

Buchenwald had one building specifically for cremating the dead. It was in fact the very building I had seen when I first arrived that blew black smoke from its thick chimney day and night. A common saying around the camp was: "The only way you leave Buchenwald was through *that* chimney."

The morning we were given that dreadful task began like every other. We had been awoken by powerful jets of cold water. Scotty, Ronald, and I filed outside with the rest of the men—whom I noticed we looked more alike in physique to with every passing day—and were designated to the crematorium.

Upon walking over to the brown brick triangular building with the ominous-looking chimney, we were hailed by a guard who broke away from a group of four others that occupied the front of the crematorium. This was the guard I had seen when I first stepped off the truck, who stood amongst his equals along the wall by the gate to Buchenwald but who did not stand as straight and proper as the others. He almost had the look in his eyes that I had come to know resided in the men with whom I was imprisoned.

"You are the Americans?" he said, though his tone did not resemble that of the other guards who seemingly took pride in shouting and expressing their superiority.

"Yes," said Scotty.

I had noticed a subtle change in Scotty ever since we arrived. His charm and good spirit had been chipping away like the gravestones we'd demolished over the past several weeks.

"Come with me," said the guard, and we followed him into the crematorium.

Inside were six large incinerators that were housed in two separate rows of three and resembled pizza ovens with heavy black semicircle cast-iron doors.

The guard unlatched the two clamps on the incinerator door closest to us and pulled on a handle that was wrapped in white cloth to protect the hand from the hot metal. Inside the incinerator, on a blackened rolling tray, were charred skeletal remains that still resembled the human figure to a disturbing degree.

A ribcage pointed upward like the legs of a dead crab on a beach, and the pelvic bone was still connected by the spine. The legs and arms lay in crumbled fragments but the skull still held its shape.

It was strange to see something that looked both so familiar yet completely alien at the same time. Again I had to force myself not to think about it too much.

The guard rolled out the tray and ashy grey powder fell to the floor.

"There is a cart outside you will use to transport the remains to a building I will show you in a few moments.

There, you will pulverize the remains until they are fine and place them in a truck. Someone else will take them from there. Any questions?"

Any questions? No one had asked us if we had any questions before.

"How do we get this stuff from here to the cart?" asked Ronald, pointing to the remains on the rolled out tray.

"I will provide you with buckets and shovels. You will fill the buckets in here and dump them into the cart. Is there anything else?

"What happens to the remains after we are done with them?" asked Scotty somberly, barely managing to bring his eyes up to the guard's face.

The guard cleared his throat. He almost looked uncomfortable.

"Most will be used as fertilizer throughout the camp. The rest will be used to make soap."

My eyes dropped to the floor as he said this.

Soap. These bastards were using the cremated remains of their prisoners to make *soap.*

"If there isn't anything else, I will show you to the building you will be going to with the cart."

The building proved to be more of a barn than a more civilized structure akin to those that dotted the grounds of the entrance to Buchenwald. Inside were long wooden tables with sheet metal covering their surfaces. The ends of the metal sheets were bent upward, creating lips to keep the remains from spilling onto the floor when crushed. A single mallet was fixed to the table with metal wire through a hole in the handle that we were to use to pulverize the bones that the incinerator had not been able to fully destroy. Against the entry wall were stacks of wooden barrels.

"Once you have reduced the remains to a powder you will fill those barrels and load them into the truck outside. Are there any questions?"

Even if we had questions, we refused to ask them as I believe we were afraid of the answers we may be given. We stirred in silence.

"Good," said the guard. "Then let us begin."

We marched back to the crematorium and began our work.

We worked with another group of prisoners who had the unfortunate job of loading up the incinerators with the dead. Each body took roughly three hours but the work was staggered in a way that we were almost always working. When a cremation had finished we would open the incinerator and slide the tray out of the chamber. We would remove the remains and fill our buckets, then take those buckets to the cart outside where we would offload the haul. Once the tray was clear, we would use our shovels to scoop out the bone fragments that had fallen from the tray from inside the incinerator and repeat the process. In stark contrast to the gravestones, bone and ash were relatively light. But the heat was brutal.

When we'd emptied all available incinerators, they would be loaded up again and we would push the cart to the barn where we would process the remains. Taking our buckets with us, we would fill them from the cart the way one retrieves water from a lake, and empty them out on an available table. Then, with our mallets, we would crush the remains.

Most of the bones that remained intact from the cremation process were easy to disregard as human once isolated from the rest of the body, but the skull was always a heartbreaking challenge. There was no way to fool yourself into thinking it was the remains of a deer, or cow, or pig. It was undeniably human.

The raised metal lip helped in keeping everything on the table, but a mallet strike was explosive by nature and fragments would be flung from the table with almost every blow. Once a relatively fine powder had been achieved, the ashes would be transferred into the wooden barrels provided and loaded into a truck. Then, the process would repeat.

There were many little annoyances that became apparent over time. The emanating heat from the incinerator chamber would cause you to sweat, the shoveling of ashes would cause the finer powder to become airborne and stick to your skin. We would look like coal miners by the end of the day.

Not only would it stick to your skin but you would inhale it. It would line your mouth and coat your teeth. It would get inside your nose and ears and eyes. When you spat, it was black.

I do not wish to describe the smell of the inside of an incinerator.

We continued this work for several days. We had assumed this cleaning process was to be done after every burn but were quickly scolded by a guard for doing so.

Instead we were ordered to merely push what remained on the rolling tray to the side to fall below so another body could take its place. And only when the chamber below filled up to where the tray could no longer roll out unobstructed were we to empty its contents.

I would learn in the following days that the guard who first described the details of our job was named August. Though I spoke no German, I would overhear conversations he would have with the other guards who monitored us, where he would respond to this name. One evening while I was crushing bone, I overheard him being addressed by a guard by another name.

Von Strauss.

My head turned and I briefly watched these men talk before the other guard caught me and barked at me to get back to work. I waited until he left and August stood in the doorway alone.

"Von Strauss," I said to see what kind of reaction I would get.

August's head shot toward me. "Yes?" he questioned, curious by my use of his last name.

I tried saying another name to see what reaction *this* might produce.

"Dieter Von Strauss."

It was effective. August marched toward me with long, powerful strides.

"Where did you get this name?" he demanded. But before I could respond he repeated the question, this time shouting, causing his voice to crack and raise several octaves on the word "name."

This all but confirmed my suspicion.

August swatted me across the face and I crumbled to the ground.

"How do you know this name, American?"

"He was my friend," I said through a groan, rising to my knees.

"Nonsense!" barked August, and shoved me with the bottom of his foot, causing me to fall sprawling on my back.

Both Scotty and Ronald looked on helplessly.

"You're his brother, aren't you?" I questioned from the ground.

"No brother of mine would befriend an *Ami!* You lie!" Another kick came down to my side. "My brother was killed in action! Do you take me for a fool? How do you know this name?!" The pummeling of kicks continued as I squirmed about on the floor.

"Your father fought in the Great War," I squawked, "as a medic! He opened a workshop to fix shoes!"

The kicking subsided.

"Who told you this?" said August, standing over me panting, but now he had a look in his eyes of reluctant acceptance and confusion.

"How do you know this?" he asked, his chest rising and falling.

"He told me. We spent weeks together. We looked out for each other. He was my friend."

"I don't believe you," he said, shaking his head and taking a few steps back almost as if he were drunk.

"He was born on the twenty-second of January. That would make him seventeen or eighteen now. I don't know the date."

August's look of fury crumbled into that of revelation.

"Is he alive?" he asked through trembling lips.

"The officer that brought me here, he killed him."

August's composure deteriorated further into a volatile sadness.

"I don't understand. Why would he be killed by a German officer?" His eyes were now bordered with red and appeared glassy.

"Because he refused to kill *me.*"

With this, August's face hardened once more and he strode out of the barn without speaking any further.

Scotty came to my side and helped me to my feet.

"You got some balls, you know?" he said, patting the dirt and ash from my back.

I did not reply but simply looked to him before looking away to the door.

Seventeen

That night I sat awake and spoke with Avenir after we had eaten our bread rations and I told him about my interaction with August.

"You're lucky he didn't kill you right then and there for speaking out of line," he said.

"I don't believe he's like the others," I replied, lying flat on my back on the hard wooden bunk with my fingers crossed over my chest.

"They're *all* like the others."

"If he's anything like his brother then he is different. What I don't understand is how he ended up in a place like this."

"I don't think there's any reasonable answer to a question like that," Avenir replied.

I pondered this in silence.

"You are sure this guy is his brother?" Avenir asked, turning to me in the bunk.

"I'm positive," I replied. "You should have seen it. He knew I was telling the truth."

Avenir sighed deeply. "So what happens now?"

"I don't know," I replied truthfully, shaking my head. "I just don't know."

"Well, if you want my advice, I wouldn't bring it up again. I've heard rumors the Americans are getting close and this will all be over soon. Keep your head down, son. Don't let something foolish like this be the end of you after all we've been through."

We said nothing more and both drifted off to sleep.

Instead of a gust of water, I was awoken by a gentle nudge. When I turned to see who had awoken me I was greeted by the face of August Von Strauss.

"I need you to come with me," he said.

I looked to Avenir beside me; he was still asleep.

"Come."

Sheepishly, I crawled out of my bunk and went outside with August where a Volkswagen sat parked. The German Volkswagen looked similar to the American Jeep in appearance, though the Volkswagen had a downward-sloping front end. He walked over to the driver's seat before seeing I stood frozen in the doorway of the block.

"Get in."

I shuffled my feet toward the vehicle and opened the passenger door. Upon sitting down, I turned to August but remained silent as he sat behind the wheel and fired up the engine.

"Where are we going?" I asked.

"Don't speak," he replied shortly and put the vehicle in gear.

We drove throughout the blocks to a fence that had a latch. August stopped the vehicle and stepped out, leaving the engine running. Lifting the latch, he swung the fence panel open and returned to the car and drove through it, then repeated the process to close it again.

We rode in silence as we got farther and farther from the camp. I figured that this was it. I was to be driven out to the middle of nowhere to be executed. But why not kill me in my bunk or have me experience a "working accident"? My mind ran like a racehorse.

After about ten minutes of driving, August spoke.

"I spoke with Hibler about the day he captured you and brought you in," he said. "He mentioned nothing about killing a German soldier."

"You can ask any one of the Americans I came with. They will tell you it happened," I pleaded.

"I don't need to. You will show me."

I don't know how long we had been driving for, but it felt like forever. The countryside was dark and still but the sounds of gunfire and explosions could faintly be heard on the wind.

The seat I was in was very comfortable compared to the hard wooden bunk I had been sleeping in for the last two and a half weeks, and at some point I fell asleep.

"We're here."

I awoke with a start, completely unaware of where I was. In the milky cones of the Volkswagen's headlights, I could see American Jeeps that rested on the right side of the curved dirt road.

"Is this the place?" August asked me.

I didn't need to look around at anything else to know that it was.

"Yes."

"The report says the deceased were placed in the ditch. Point it out to me."

I pointed to the spot where I thought Dieter lay.

August killed the engine and stepped out from the vehicle. He walked over to look and swiftly returned, retrieving his sidearm from its holster.

"Get out," he barked at me.

"He's there!" I cried.

"Nonsense! All I see are American uniforms!"

"Check the one with the coat over his face!" I protested as August ripped the door open and held me at gunpoint.

"Check him! Just check him!"

"Why would he be in American uniform?" he demanded.

"Just look! Check his front-right pocket. You'll find a white cloth."

August lowered his weapon swiftly and marched back over to the ditch. This time he spent a lot longer doing his examination.

After some time he sauntered back to me, his sidearm back in its holster, a deflated man with a square of white cloth in his hands.

"Help me carry him," he said, and I did as he asked.

We returned to Buchenwald and placed Dieter in one of the camp's incinerators and sat inside the crematorium against the wall with our arms resting on our knees as we waited for the cremation to complete.

"I cannot do this anymore," said August as he stared idly at the incinerator's black cast-iron door. "How can anyone make sense of all this?"

I didn't reply, instead choosing to let him speak.

"I thought I understood why this needed to happen. I knew it to be wrong, but it was what I was told to do. I obeyed every order without question. I was efficient and proud to serve my country, but then it all spiraled out of control. I have tried to tell myself there is purpose and meaning behind what I do but the curtain was lifted long ago."

"Why don't you leave?" I asked.

"And have them go after my family? No. I am also a prisoner here, just in another way."

Both of us remained transfixed on the incinerator door.

"Tell me of my brother. Tell me what your time with him was like," said August, who actually turned to face me.

So I did.

I told him of our first encounter in the farmhouse and fleeing into the woods. I spoke about how he made sure we stopped often so I could warm my feet by a fire. Of the family that took us in. Of his illness, and of Hammes.

August would smile as I recounted our endeavors, though his eyes remained sad.

"You were brave to do that," he said when I mentioned how I had retrieved the door from the ruins of a crumbled building to carry Dieter to Hammes' cellar.

When I had finished the tale of my journey with Dieter, August shared some of his own and before I knew it we weren't just sharing stories, we were sharing eulogies about a man we both admired deeply.

The time seemed to flow by at this point. We weren't speaking as guard and inmate, but as men brought together in reminiscing over a mutual friend who had passed on. It was lovely.

When the cremation had completed, August took the cloth from his coat that I had left in Dieter's pocket and placed some of Dieter's remains inside of it.

"This may bring my parents some closure," he said, before wrapping the cloth into a ball and putting it into one of the pouches on his belt.

There was a pause for a brief moment. August shifted his shoulders. "I will meet you here in the morning. I have a plan."

Eighteen

I slept little before our morning firehose alarm clock and stumbled outside into the light of day with all the others. As I was waiting for Scotty and Ronald to emerge, I saw Tom and Barney, the two medics, arriving at the block.

"Hey, guys," I said. "It's been a while." But neither man returned my greeting.

When they got closer I saw the completely mute, robotic faces they bore. It looked as if every muscle in their faces had been severed and their features hung loosely on their skulls.

"You guys OK?" I asked, concerned.

Barney's eyes shifted toward mine then back in front of him.

They entered the block, squeezing through the flow of prisoners and vanished.

"Christ, you see them?" said Scotty as he emerged from the group of thin bodies.

"Yeah. I wonder where they have been," I replied.

"No idea. Where's Ronald?" asked Scotty.

"Haven't seen him yet."

"Hmm."

We both waited for the doorway to clear before going to check on him. He was dead.

As we stood by his bunk I heard Barney speak up from somewhere behind me.

"He's lucky," he said, and both Scotty and I turned to face him. He was blank and emotionless.

"You should see what kind of experiments they do here. Going in your sleep ain't so bad. Good night."

Barney climbed into his bunk and placed a striped shirt over his face.

Scotty and I walked down to the crematorium as we had for the last several days where August was awaiting our arrival.

"Where's the other one?" he said as we approached.

Scotty just shook his head and brushed past him. August followed him with his head before turning to me.

"He passed in the night," I said, grimly.

"I will request a replacement," August replied.

I nodded and went to enter the building but was stopped by August with a hand on my bicep.

"Spill a bucket so I can reprimand you. We will speak then."

"You do realize what's *in* those buckets."

"All too well. Do it."

With that, I began my duty of checking available incinerators to see which of them needed emptying. None seemed full enough so I chose the one that was fullest.

I shoveled out the charred remains into my bucket and carried it out to the cart along with Scotty. After the incinerator was nearly empty, I let the bucket slip from my hands to the floor. Ash and bone fragments scattered everywhere. August came swooping in and began the theatre.

"You there! What the hell have you done?"

The other guards who stood outside swiveled their heads to look at the commotion.

I chose not to speak and let August control the scene.

"You!" he barked at Scotty. "Clean this up. You!" He pointed at me. "Come with me." He marched over and grasped my upper arm and hauled me from the crematorium. The other guards watched with slimy grins on their faces. They called to him in German words I did not understand as August escorted me away from the building.

He took me to the barn where we crushed the remains and closed the door behind him. He let go of my arm.

"I apologize if I hurt you," he said as he realized I was rubbing my shoulder.

"It's fine. What is this all about?"

August pulled a slip of paper from his coat and splayed it open on the ashy table.

"This is a map with the location of Buchenwald, as well as every other camp in Europe."

147

The map spanned from the shores of France to the Black Sea. On it were several red dots indicating German labor camps and black dots indicating death camps. It was littered with what looked like hand-drawn scribbles of lines and boxes and arrows.

"There are that many?" I questioned, seeing hundreds of dots litter the map like mold spots.

"This is why you must do what I ask of you."

In the beginning of this tale I said that I felt no shame in abandoning the war, for I did not know the reason for my fighting.

I knew the enemy must be stopped but I hadn't known *this*. All across German-controlled Europe places like Buchenwald existed. Buchenwald held nearly 80,000 prisoners, and that was only one camp. This map seemingly indicated hundreds. *This* is why we were fighting. To end this oppressive cruelty carried out by an unfeeling foe.

Now I felt shame. Great shame by running away from an enemy of such malice and allowing places like *this* to operate by my cowardice.

"What would you have me do?" I asked, feeling a rush of determination and retribution.

August pointed to a spot on the map that had been circled just past the Netherlands border.

"Your forces have managed to capture the town of Asten, south of Nijmegen, in their push towards Germany. Ideally I was hoping for somewhere closer but this should have you avoid the larger fighting."

"I don't understand," I said, looking up to him after he finished tracing his finger along a broken line that led from where we were to the circled town of Asten.

August began to fold the map back up and hand it to me. "Like last night, I will wake you. I will drive you as far as I can but you will have to go most of the way on foot."

I began to speak but August continued. "Get this map to your men. Make sure they find these camps."

A momentous heaviness fell over me.

"How . . . how far is it?"

"By vehicle, maybe half a day. On foot, a week, if you keep rest to a minimum."

His expression shared the daunting weight I felt as he said this.

"I can drive you about an hour out but that's all I can do. You have to get this map to your men, do you understand?"

I did. As much of a burden I felt I was undertaking, I understood it perfectly clearly.

"Tonight?" I asked.

"Tonight," he reaffirmed. "I will get you as much food and supplies as I can, but this is all I can do."

I ran everything over in my mind. I would have to go back into the elements. Even when I had considerably more weight on my bones it had been unrelenting. Now it seemed next to impossible. But I had to try.

"OK," I said. "Tonight."

We both leaned against the table in silence, contemplating the task ahead.

"I'll have to rough you up a bit to show the guards I punished you for dropping that bucket."

I closed my eyes and let out a deep sigh before standing up straight, chin out.

"Make it quick."

We walked back to the crematorium, August holding me by the collar of my shirt with the map tucked into my waistband. The guards laughed at my bloody nose and swelling eye.

The pile of ash had been removed from the floor and sprawling finger lines remained in arcs. When Scotty saw me he quickly lowered his head and went back to shoveling inside the incinerator chamber. August shoved me in through the door and went to regroup with the other guards who stood watch out front.

I retrieved my shovel and stood opposite Scotty and shoved the spade into the chamber.

"Jesus, you all right?" asked Scotty. "What did he do to you?" His eyes ran all over my bruising face.

"We'll speak later, OK?"

"Of course."

We worked for the rest of the day.

Come nightfall, we returned to Block 40 to find it empty. I told Scotty everything.

"You gotta take me with you," he said in the pitch black.

"It's not up to me, Scotty."

"Well, I'll stay up with you and talk to him when he gets here."

"OK," I nodded. "But I don't know if I was supposed to tell anyone. So this stays between us."

"Who the hell am I going to tell? I don't speak German."

"Just keep it to yourself, OK?"

"Yeah, yeah, of course. I can't believe we're getting out of here. We'll probably get medals for this!"

His enthusiasm was welcomed but I remained cautious.

"I'm going to lie down for a bit. You should do the same," I said.

"There's no way I'm getting any sleep. Shit, it's like Christmas Eve."

I think we were both out before we were fully in our bunks.

I was awoken not by the chill of cold water or the rustle of August's hands but from an internal nervousness that demanded my immediate attention. I looked around to find my fellow prisoners still asleep in their bunks as the light of morning crept in through the gaps in the walls.

A dull panic resided within me and I looked to Scotty, who was also sleeping quietly.

Why wasn't I awoken in the night? Had something happened? Tendrils of unease licked my body all over.

As my mind pondered all the crushing possibilities of August's absence, I heard the door of Block 40 swing open and the water began to flow.

Scotty and I walked over to the crematorium hurling rhetorical questions at one another that neither of us had the answers to.

Why hadn't he shown?

Could he be trusted after all?

Do you think he had been caught?

Our spirits were low and bothered.

We arrived at the crematorium to see the usual cluster of guards, though August was not among them.

"You look one man short," said Scotty to the group of guards who were talking amongst themselves. "Did he take a vacation day or something?"

I feared he would be beaten for speaking to the guards in this way but one of them turned to address him.

"Working accident," said the guard and spat dryly into the dirt.

I saw Scotty swing his head toward me but I kept mine down like a scolded dog. I knew all too well what a "working accident" meant.

We shuffled into the building and got to work.

We spoke little throughout the day. Scotty tried raising questions about what might have happened to August but I did not entertain them.

"Not now," I would hiss and he would reserve further prodding.

I thought about what they might have done to August. He surely had been caught, but how? Was he seen procuring extra rations for me? Had he been caught trying to slip away in the night? Formulating these scenarios did me no good, but I was helpless to stop them from playing in my mind like a film projector.

Your sacrifice will not be for nothing.

After half a day of shoveling and crushing, a wide-eyed prisoner was thrown in through the door of the crematorium. He had the expression of a rabbit in a snare and Scotty and I lowered our shovels.

"Who's this?" said Scotty, again, it seemed to me, pushing his luck with the guards.

"Replacement," the guard who had delivered him said before turning and walking away.

The man stood petrified as his eyes soaked up the six large incinerators.

We did not ask his name, for we did not care in our deflated state. He spoke no English so we were forced to show him everything by example. He picked it up quickly and we worked until sundown.

Lying awake in my bunk, I could hear the shuffling sound of many feet approaching the block. The door gently opened and those who had been assigned to the quarry came sauntering in. They climbed into their bunks with bread rations in hand and settled.

"They have you working later," I said to Avenir as he crawled in beside me.

"More and more men keep collapsing. We must complete their work as well as our own."

"How many men are working at the quarry?" I asked.

"Hundreds," Avenir replied. "They bring more, and more die. A vicious cycle."

A thought came into my head.

"How many guards are there?"

"Twelve, maybe."

"And you all have tools?"

"I see what you're getting at, son," Avenir said cautiously. "But what good would that do? Many would be shot and killed."

I slid the map from my waistband—as I kept it on me at all times—and held it out to him.

"Unless that's a picture of Greta Garbo I don't care to see it," he mumbled sleepily.

"It's a map," I retorted, "of every labor camp in Germany. Europe, too."

Though very dark, my eyes had adjusted.

Avenir turned to me with a sharp pivot of the head.

"Where did you get this?!" he whispered, though with urgency.

"One of the guards. I need to get it to the Americans. They will come."

Avenir seemed out of breath, almost panting.

"The other night he came to me. He wants this to end, as well. He was supposed to smuggle me out of here but I fear he was discovered."

"And they haven't come for you yet?" he asked.

"No."

Avenir lay flat again and massaged his hollow cheeks with an index finger and thumb.

"You need a diversion," he said quietly, stating it rather than asking.

"If you can cause a revolt, it may pull the guards away to the quarry. It may give me a chance."

"We will be slaughtered," said Avenir, grimly.

I let his words hang in the air for a moment before speaking.

"Yes," I agreed.

"How sure are you that you could get out?" he asked.

"I know of a gate. I can get there."

Avenir lay in silence. I could almost hear his mind whirring.

After some time, he spoke.

"It will be done," he said. "I'll need time to speak with the men. We will talk more tomorrow night."

"OK."

Nineteen

Scotty and I spoke about my conversation with Avenir throughout the following day only when we were not under direct supervision. It was rare but there were gaps here and there. I told him of Avenir's plan to overwhelm the guards who roamed the quarry in hopes to attract attention throughout the camp. I told him of the gate August had shown me from which escape seemed the most plausible.

While we walked back from the barn with our empty cart, I pointed it out to him across the courtyard. Two guards stood watch to either side of it, but if Avenir and his men could cause enough of a stir then hopefully they would abandon their posts to aid their fellow guardsmen. It may have been a longshot but it was the only one I had.

"You think it will work?" asked Scotty, his face black with ash.

"It has to," I replied, unable to take my eyes off that gate.

Back in our block, I awaited Avenir's return. When he finally managed to stumble in I looked to him with hopeful eyes.

"Tomorrow," he said, "just after dark. That's when we will do it."

I felt an immense weight lift from my chest only to be replaced by another. This was actually to happen, then it was all on me.

Tomorrow was the day.

I was filled with anxiety from the instant I was awoken from the gushing of pressurized water. I shook Avenir's hand and we shared a few words.

"I wish you luck, my friend," I said, finding it hard to separate, knowing it was likely the last time I would ever see him.

"Move fast, and hard. This cannot be for nothing," he replied.

"I will. Do you have any family I can contact?" I asked, feeling a catch in my throat.

"They are all gone," he said through a somber smile, and patted my cheek while looking up to my face with warm, soft eyes. "There is nothing left for me in this world, but I look forward to seeing them in the next."

I sniffed and continuously cleared my throat to keep my composure. But even if I were to cry, my tears would be indistinguishable from the rest of the water that dripped from my head from our ritual icy awakenings.

"But there are men here who do have wives and children waiting for them beyond this place," he continued. "Make sure they get home to them."

With that, he turned and joined the group that amassed outside the block and I watched him disappear in the crowd.

Scotty and I worked that day but our minds were somewhere else. We would watch as the sun crossed the sky on its primordial arc and seemed to count the seconds until it plunged back into the earth. I could not stop my hands from shaking.

When it finally made its graceful bow behind the trees, all we could do was wait.

We were in the crematorium when it began and the first guard was seen dashing across the courtyard. Then another, and another. Now vehicles full of German guards whizzed past, causing great plumes of dust to arise and swirl behind them. That was when the alarm began to ring. It boomed with sharp, braying repetition and a voice spewed hurried words through speakers that stood clustered atop tall poles from which tangles of wires hung. I shot my head through the doorway of the crematorium to look across the courtyard to the gate where the two German guards who were positioned there began to sprint away in the direction of the quarry.

The guards who stood watch over us also scampered toward the quarry, whence yelling and gunshots could now be heard echoing.

"It's happening!" I barked to Scotty and we rushed out of the building to the frozen bewilderment of the wide-eyed replacement.

Just as we had emerged from the crematorium, Scotty split off to the left, away from the direction of the gate.

"Where are you going?!" I yelled in confusion.

"Get to the gate, I'll meet you there!"

There was no time for questions, no matter how many rattled throughout my brain.

I made my way to the blocks, hoping to use them to stay out of sight from the guards who were now coming from all over. I slunk in between buildings, stopping only to check for a clear path of advancement before pushing forward. Those who remained in their blocks came pouring out slowly to see what the commotion was about. Those who understood the voice coming from the speakers rushed toward the quarry, perhaps to aid their fellow prisoners, perhaps to exact some form of retribution. Some collapsed in terror while others simply went back inside.

The earlier spats of gunfire and hollering had now seemed to grow into a full-blown roar of confrontation. A battle was surely erupting.

I could now see trucks full of guards careening toward the fight as opposed to the smaller Volkswagens that had begun the frantic defense. With all that firepower, the tide would be turning soon. It would be a massacre.

Emerging from the blocks, I saw the gate was now in sight. I was exhausted. I could collapse at any moment, but I had to press on. For Avenir, for these men so cruelly imprisoned, for August, for Dieter. I could not stop now.

My body bounced off the gate as I reached it in my unflinching momentum. I fumbled with the latch and pulled the panel toward me. Regardless of its hinges, it was still hard to get it into motion with my famished arms, but once it began to swing, I cast it aside and slid through. This was it. I was *free*.

"Halt!" A voice beckoned from behind me and I stopped dead in my tracks. For a complete lack of what to do I stood frozen in place, petrified. The ground erupted to my left as a shot was fired and I cowered away from it and threw my hands in the air. Another explosion of dirt and rock came in on my right, spitting soil into my face.

He was toying with me.

I turned slowly and the lonesome guard who stood in the open gate fired again at my feet, chuckling to himself. My hands sprang in front of my face to shield it from the debris. He began casually walking toward me with a swagger in his step, firing bullets into the ground at my feet before raising his rifle and I was struck in the arm. I crumbled to the ground as a burning hot pain enveloped me.

This can't be how it ends.

The guard stood over me and watched me writhe with pain before spitting on me.

"So close," he said, and brought the barrel of his rifle up to my head.

I raised my eyes to face him in a defiance I did not know I had and saw a flash of movement behind him, then there was a *clang*.

The guard toppled over top of me, his rifle tumbling from his hands, and I managed to scurry out from underneath him. As I gained a little distance, I saw Scotty standing above him, the mallet we had used to pulverize the prisoner's remains in his hand. He raised his arm and swung it down again on top of the guards helmet and it rolled from his head. Dazed but not out, the guard grabbed Scotty's legs and brought him to the ground, where they began to tussle.

"Go!" Scotty yelled, and, without missing a beat, I did so. I moved fast and hard despite the throbbing in my arm.

Just like in training I ran and ran, then I ran some more.

PART III:

NO GOOD DEED

"You don't ask people with knives in their stomachs
what would make them happy; happiness is no longer
the point. It's all about survival; it's all about whether you
pull the knife out and bleed to death or keep it in. . . ."
-Nick Hornby

Twenty

As I ran, I slid the map from my waistband for two reasons. One: so it would not slide down my pant leg, out the bottom, and be lost forever. And two: I was bleeding. The entirety of my sleeve below the elbow on my right arm was now red with blood and stuck to my skin. I did not want to have the map ruined and unreadable by my clipped wing.

The sounds of the uprising began to grow distant and I slung myself into a nearby ditch to rest a moment and assess the damage. I needed to lower my heart rate as its accelerated pace only rushed the bleeding further.

Thankfully, the ground was dry and I placed the map to the side and began to roll up my sleeve. This proved too painful so instead I unbuttoned my shirt and freed my arm that way.

Just above the elbow in the crook of my arm was the most recognizable injury during the war: a bullet hole. I pivoted my elbow to search for an exit wound but found none. The bullet hadn't blown through.

To my horror, I realized that my bicep was *gone*. It hadn't been blown away by the gunshot but no longer resided under the skin where it should be. Instead, it had recoiled up my arm and sat near my armpit in a lump. Seeing this filled me with a sickly revulsion even more than the bullet hole itself.

I continued removing my shirt with some difficulties and bunched it into my hand. After a few quick breaths in preparation, I pressed it to the wound and applied pressure.

I grimaced in pain but remained quiet, regardless of how much I wanted to scream. I lay back in the grassy ditch as my eyes rolled and my teeth clenched. I began to focus on my breathing in an attempt to lower my frantic heart rate and soon it subsided.

It was dark and cold but this did not warrant my immediate attention. My only priority was to stop the bleeding. I would check the wound periodically to see if clotting had been achieved. The first several times, the hole in my arm would immediately begin to fill with blood as soon as the shirt was removed. More pressure.

After some time, the bleeding had slowed to where I was satisfied enough to move on. I tied my shirt around my arm for a bandage and let the excess hang. If I wasn't to come across a body from which I could pillage a uniform, then I could put the shirt back on if needed.

"*A week,*" August had said. So far I'd made it less than an hour and had already sustained a potentially life-threatening injury. I had to keep moving.

I gathered the map in my good hand, shirtless and cold, and pressed on.

According to the map, the Germans were in retreat as indicated with hand-drawn arrows pointing back toward Germany. A solid line ran from top to bottom of the visible European continent from Westkapelle, Netherlands, to Colmar, France. It was less of a line and more of a jagged, slinking trail like that left by a slug. This line was thicker than all the others, and accompanied by clusters of squares that I assumed indicated where battalions were fighting. The empty boxes were ours, the filled-in boxes were German.

I wasn't sure if August had marked this map himself, though I assumed he had as the markings lacked much of the detailed information you would normally see if the map had come down from the higher-ups. But the only information I needed was the broken line that ran from Buchenwald to Asten.

My next stop seemed to be a town by the name of Erfurt, followed by the town of Gotha. That was all I needed to know for now. I just hoped I found a fallen soldier for clothing or, God willing, a running vehicle by then.

I was overjoyed, or as close as one could get given the circumstances, by the lack of snow on the ground. I could walk freely without the hindrance of removing myself every few steps from its misleading depths. I was cold, yes, but my steady pace helped in that regard.

Plumes of hot air left my mouth and wrapped around my head as I went. Like before, I stuck close to the road while managing to keep distance in case of anyone passing by. But maybe that was what I needed, the good grace of a stranger. But I felt I had spent all my luck getting this far and was unsure if I could recoup my losses on a bad bet.

The moon hung in the sky like a watchtower spotlight—the only reference that was fresh in my mind. The land around me was mostly flat, which filled me with an anxiety I had only felt under the immediate threat of mortar fire. But instead of mortars it was eyes I prayed would never fall upon me. They may prove just as deadly.

Though I was moving quickly, you could never truly outrun the cold. My pores would fill with sweat as my body warmed from exertion, then that sweat would seem to freeze in the late night air, immersing me in an impenetrable cold with which I was all too familiar.

I had had no water all day. Perhaps the only benefit to the snow was you could boil it down to drink or simply shove a handful of the stuff in your mouth and suck on it. The last few days had produced no rain either. I figured I could lap from puddles like a dog but I would have to wait for that opportunity.

How big was Erfurt? The map presented it as a point into which many roads converged. It looked like a spider's web or a fractured pane of glass with cracks expanding outward from a single impact. Was it a town or a *city*? A *city* meant a lot of people. A lot of people meant transportation. Transportation meant success. For the time being, I had to forget Asten. Erfurt was the goal.

It was still dark when my body decided it needed to rest. My limbs were weak and I began to become light-headed as I trudged along through the German countryside. My body gave me no time to prepare any kind of place to rest as my legs refused to take me any farther. A vicious nausea swept over me and I felt I may vomit if I didn't lie down. My surroundings were mostly clear with little in the way of cover or foliage, so I merely collapsed into the grass where I stood. I closed my eyes and managed my breathing in an attempt to combat my nausea. I did not want to vomit despite every attempt my body was making to do so. I lay flat under a starless sky completely motion-less for maybe three minutes before passing into sleep.

I was awoken by a strange tingling feeling on my face. When my eyes opened I was greeted by the snout of a dog as it licked my cracked lips.

The sight startled me and I scurried backward in the dewy grass, which also seemed to startle the dog, who lurched away defensively.

I went to wipe my mouth in the golden early morning light but a sharp, striking pain reminded me that my arm of choice was out of commission. I used my other hand instead.

The dog began to reluctantly creep back toward me with its nose low to the ground and its eyes turned up, observing me, cautiously.

"Go on, get!" I demanded with a wave of the arm and the dog hopped backward in the grass and dropped to the ground on its two front paws, its hindquarters still up in the air, with playful, expecting eyes.

"No. Back!"

Its tail wagged as if this were some kind of game.

I pretended to lunge forward and it sprang back up on all fours and began to hop around in excited circles, barking.

"Go on!"

The dog turned and zipped off with great speed. I envied its energy and agility.

As my excitement from this encounter wore off, the cold crept back in. I rose stiffly and spent no more time in getting moving.

The sun wasn't quite in the sky just yet but its light was the sign of another day, and that was welcome. It was chilly and the wind seemed to be picking up. Soon it began to blow heavily, causing the freshly thawed grass to wave in mesmerizing pulses and push the small bushes that dotted the countryside around like the bully it was. I found myself conjuring low, beastly grunts in response. My muscles tensed, my nose ran, and my feet hurt. *Everything* seemed to hurt despite the numbing cold the wind brought with it.

My right arm hung loosely from my body, utterly useless and swayed with every step. I was only able to move my thumb, and my index and middle fingers; my ring finger and pinky stubbornly refused to comply.

As I stumbled along like a sleepwalker, I contemplated the nastiness of a bullet. It was such a crude and devastating invention. There were few other things made by man with the sole purpose to destroy. Even a firearm was mostly harmless without this small, almost insignificant piece of metal. A sword you swing. A bayonet you thrust. But all it takes to harness the power of the humble bullet is a flinch of the finger. In the history of humankind it has never been so easy to take a life, nor has it been so terrifyingly accessible. The bullet in my arm undoubtedly had shattered my elbow. It severed my bicep and rendered my fingers inert. And all within a fraction of a second. I know not with what weapons our next war will be fought with, but the one that follows will surely be fought with sticks and stones.

It was hard to believe I was walking through the land of the enemy. In truth, it looked a lot like home. The grass was green, the sky was blue, the trees swayed the same way in the wind. I don't know why I expected different. How could something beautiful exist in the land of the most vile enemy the world had ever seen? Somehow I expected to see nothing but concrete and steel bars, fire and smokestacks. But what surrounded me was land untouched by war. The trees had not been chewed up by gunfire and reduced to splinters. The ground was free of fox holes and mortar craters. You could hear birds chirping away and singing their morning songs. No dead lay strewn across the field before me in sickly contortions. No blood, no yelling, no stench of decay and death. Here, I was the only thing that signified a war was even being fought.

I began to come across signs of civilization in the form of farmhouses that sprouted up around me like dandelions in summer. They were mostly neglected in appearance but harbored livestock within rickety fences. Cows grazed lethargically on long, moist blades of grass and chickens could be heard clucking in their pens. There was life here, but if these people had been fed the same sort of hyperbolic propaganda of *us* that we had seen back home of *them* then I thought it best to avoid all contact, if possible. It's true that I may not be visibly recognizable as American on sight, but given my current famished state, my arm caked with blood, and my striped uniform, I would surely be recognized as some sort of representative of war, and perhaps that was reason enough to be wary of me.

Regardless, I slipped through the fence of the first farmhouse I came across with a chicken coop and retrieved several eggs. The first two I cracked open and swallowed right there on the spot, the others I took with me in a bucket that most likely had been used for collecting milk whose bottom I lined with dry grass and sawdust.

Every so often I would turn to see that damn dog lurking behind me a distance. When it saw me pivot its way, it would lay prone in the grass, resting its head between its forward paws on the ground and stare as if this position completely concealed its presence.

It was a medium-sized dog, mostly blonde in color with darker patches mixed in. It had a great fluffy tail with a white tip and long, wispy tassels flowing from the back of its legs that flowed in the wind. If I had to guess, I'd say it was some sort of Shepherd mix, perhaps with some Husky in there. It was a beautiful-looking dog.

Within twenty minutes, my stomach began to tie itself in knots. I had eaten another two eggs in this time and it seemed as though the sudden intake of calories and protein was not sitting well with my empty belly.

I sat my bucket down and curled into a ball on the ground as if struck in the abdomen by a bullet. My toes curled and splayed from the pain. Again, I was fighting the urge to vomit. I knew it would most likely make me feel better but I did not want to rid myself of the fuel those eggs would provide.

The dog approached me again and began sniffing at my crudely bandaged arm.

"No," I said weakly, waving it away, but it seemed to have a laser-beam focus on my wound.

I took an egg from the bucket and let the dog sniff it curiously. Then I lobbed it a distance and it landed with a *splat*. The dog trotted after it and began licking the splattered egg from the ground.

Finally, I got to a point where vomiting was unavoidable and heaved up everything I had in me. Once finished, I was relieved to find the pain in my belly was gone.

The dog returned as I began to sit up and brought its nose to my bandage once again like a magnet.

"It's infected, isn't it?" I said to the dog and it looked up to me briefly before returning to the spoiled wrap around my arm.

I leaned back and determined this dog was male. I looked for a collar but found none.

"Would you mind delivering a piece of paper for me?" I asked the dog, if only to entertain myself. "I think you'd get it there faster than I could."

The dog kept sniffing.

"Oh, you could do that for me? That would be great. It's a map, so it's not like you can get lost. The path is even marked and everything."

I pretended as if the dog had responded.

"A town called Asten. Yeah, I've never heard of it either."

The dog seemingly reacted to something I had said by looking me in the eyes and twisting his head in that adorable way dogs are known to do.

I began relaying words I had previously said to try and duplicate this reaction.

"Either." Nothing.

"Heard." Still nothing.

"Asten." The dog twisted his head the opposite way, causing his ears the flop from one side to the other. It was cute.

"All right," I said. "Asten it is."

I spoke casually to Asten as he trotted along beside me. I found it helped to ease my worried mind.

"Can you believe that?" I said. "She was ten years older than he was."

Asten walked alongside me with his tongue hanging from his open mouth, his breath producing plumes like mine.

"Yeah, it was hard not to like him. I don't blame her, either."

I began to feel the sprinkling of rain on my bare shoulders. I extended my open palm out in front of me.

"Looks like rain's coming," I said. "Let's sit for a minute. I'm going to put my shirt back on."

I found a spot to sit as the rain began to pick up and emptied the bucket of eggs onto the ground. I sat the bucket beside me in hopes it would collect some water for drinking and started to loosen the bandage around my arm. Asten immediately sprang to my side and began sniffing the spot I had been shot again.

Once I had the shirt that I had repurposed into a bandage undone, it stuck to the wound as I tried to remove it.

Slowly, I peeled it from my skin.

Once I'd removed it, Asten tried to lick the exposed wound and I shoved his snout away. Looking at the hole in my arm, I could see it was moist with a yellowish puss.

I looked to Asten, who looked back at me with anticipation.

"Well, go on then."

Asten jumped at the opportunity he had been itching for since we met and began licking feverishly at the infection.

"Gentle!" I grunted, as the licking was painful, and as if adhering to my command, Asten slowed his pace and continued to seemingly feast on my arm with a gentle tongue.

He did a damn good job. In the span of minutes, the puss had been cleared and the perfect little hole looked clean.

The rain continued to fall, blown sideways with the wind, and a small amount had gathered in the bottom of my bucket. When I was ready to move on, I carefully slid my arm back into the sleeve of my shirt before doing the same with the other. The buttons proved too difficult to manage so I left the shirt hanging open.

I took the bucket and gulped down the small amount of water it had gathered before placing the eggs back inside, leaving the dry grass and sawdust where they lay.

The water was immensely refreshing and my body craved more. I licked my lips clean and got to my feet.

"All right, boy. Let's go."

Every so often, Asten would shake the rain from his fur, which would cast it off and onto me.

"Oh, thanks for that," I would say, already soaked to the core myself.

It was no longer a light sprinkling, but had turned into more of a miserable downpour. I shook compulsively, though I did not let it slow my pace. I kept on, defiantly, through the weather. I had done this before. I had gotten to know cold intimately. This was nothing.

My bucket would fill and I would drink. Asten licked at forming puddles as we marched along and seemed unperturbed by the conditions. Hell, he even seemed to enjoy them. I envied that about him.

After another long, grueling stretch of non-stop walking, I was sure I could see our destination. Structures began to emerge in the distance. Tall and pointed spires towered above them. This, undoubtedly, was Erfurt.

As we got closer, the size of this town became apparent. This was truly no town at all, but a hefty and sprawling city.

Erfurt looked Medieval in appearance. Like some great walled-off fortress from the time of kings and iron. The buildings were long, conjoined rows of rectangular houses of differing colors, adorned with dark wooden trim that shaped in boxes and Xs on their exteriors, with steep, angular roofs of red tile. Flat dormers seemed to rise out from these roofs as if the windows themselves were peeking out from trapdoors and thin, little chimneys stood beside them.

The road leading into Erfurt went from gravel to cobblestone and a creek carelessly flowed by, noiselessly.

I sprang for the creek and brought my lips to its surface and drank until I could not drink any more. Asten strolled up and joined me.

Once finished, I threw my head back, gasping for air as water ran down my chin and was absorbed by my already impregnated shirt. I watched as Asten drank for some time, his tongue lapping up the creek water. One, two, three, pause. One, two, three, pause, without skipping a beat. When he was finished, running his tongue over his whiskers, I looked at him, amazed.

"You were pretty thirsty, too, huh?"

He shook again and showered me with water.

Twenty-One

I decided to take a wide berth around the city of Erfurt. The city itself seemed alive and bustling with people rushing across narrow cobblestone streets, going about their business. It was as if they did not realize that only hours away a war was being fought. I had no intention of reminding them.

Asten obediently followed behind me as I slunk from the shallow recess of the creek's shore to a dense row of trees that lined the road heading into the city. It was now midday and, despite the dark, cloudy skies overhead, it was way too bright to enter the city unnoticed. I would either have to wait until dark, find a more secluded point of entry, or simply move on.

Ultimately, I figured the latter to be the optimal choice, despite this city containing everything I would need to aid me in my journey. It was just too risky given the time of day.

"Come on, boy," I said, which produced a wag of his fluffy tail, and we marched on around Erfurt, leaving my current best chance at survival behind.

More farmhouses and smaller clusters of dwellings greeted us as we pressed on through the pristine Germany countryside. We seemed to be entering more versatile terrain as gentle hills rose from the horizon and babbling creeks cut through the untouched fields before me. Some of these farmhouses had clotheslines running from porches to fence lines, but none bore any clothing due to the rain. At least the wind had died down. Now the rain fell in perfect vertical lines.

There were barns along the way we could have dipped into for cover, but what was the point? The quicker we got to Asten, the better. I would suffer, and I would be miserable, but that seemed to be the cost. That is what I had to accept to hopefully bring an end to the suffering and misery of so many others. And once I had accepted this, it was easier to go on.

I cracked open another egg, this time only sucking the yolk from the shell, and let Asten lick at the whites. My stomach still ached from time to time but it was manageable, and nowhere near as bad as it had been before.

I began to merely exist. My body shivered relentlessly. I hurt all over but I sort of became numb to it all. My head drooped forward, my shoulders hunched down, but I had found a rhythm that pushed me forward.

As we got closer to Gotha, the visible signs of war began to present themselves. Craters scarred the ground where bombing runs had occurred. Vehicles sat on country roads unattended. It gave the impression we were walking into hell, which by all accounts, we were. It was then I found it unfair for Asten to continue on with me much further.

Up ahead I saw a sign indicating *Tüttleben, 2km,* and I followed the road despite my discomfort of being so exposed. Upon reaching Tüttleben, I was relieved to find it wasn't more than a few streets lined with houses.

We walked the perimeter of the small town, where no one seemed to be outside, wisely choosing to stay indoors and out of the rain, unlike me.

Bordering the town, while keeping low and out of sight, I came across a truck parked near a home that sat on the edge of town. In the back were tools such as shovels and hoes tied down to a wooden rack with rope.

I undid the rope, but not before checking to see if the truck was unlocked. It wasn't. I tied a loop to fit around Asten's neck. He protested this vehemently. Once I had it on, I guided him to the backyard of the home where an awning provided cover from the rain and tied him off to one of the supporting beams.

"You'll be better off here, buddy," I said, as he looked at me with eyes of betrayal.

I rubbed his head and managed to muster a smile.

"Trust me, you don't want to come with me where I have to go."

I tried to make it quick, like removing a Band-Aid. I turned on my heels and made off.

Asten began barking loudly but I refused to turn to look at him. I had only been with him the better part of a day but his presence had undeniably aided my spirits.

War was no place for a pure soul. This was what was best, but it didn't make me feel any better about it.

I reached Gotha, which lay before me in ruins. The German town was apocalyptic in appearance. Some buildings had been stripped down to their skeletal framing, while others were nothing more than heaps of scorched brick. Mounds of rubble lined the streets with crooked and bent steel beams protruding from them, pointing to the sky defiantly. Trees stood black and without limbs, and corpses—shriveled and twisted—lay strewn across the muddy ground, charred and stiff.

It appeared I had stumbled onto some kind of airfield where the hollowed shells of planes dotted the strip. It looked like a graveyard of mechanical carcasses. There was nothing here of use so I wandered for a while.

After some time of seemingly aimless dawdling, I came across a residential district that had fared much better than where I had entered the town of Gotha from, yet it still shared the feeling of a complete lack of life.

I walked through the streets as if in a dream without emotion or purpose—seeing such death and destruction tends to have that effect on a person—and heard the rumble of an engine. Instinctively, I scurried from the street like a startled doe at the sound of a snapping twig and took cover in a narrow alley between houses.

I watched with wide eyes as a Volkswagen Beetle putted up the road, passed me, and came to a stop about three houses up.

A man spilled from the vehicle with a bottle in his hand and slammed the car door behind him with his foot. He was an older man, his hair peppered with grey around the temples, and was dressed in civilian clothes, but he wore the face of a soldier coming back from the line.

I followed him with cautious eyes as he crossed the road to the door of a house and fumbled with his keys in the lock. The keys slipped from his clumsy hands and fell between his feet with a *jingle,* and he hunched over to retrieve them.

As I watched him struggle, my dazed stupor started to fade and my focus began to crystallize into a hard point.

Once he had managed to make it in through the door, I swiftly took off down the alleyway, which connected to an adjacent road that ran along the back of the houses.

I skipped along, pressing my body flat against the homes behind me and found the house he entered. Looking up, I spotted a window just above my head and began scanning for things within the vicinity to stand upon, ultimately using my bucket, which I placed upside down on the ground and balanced atop.

As I straightened to peek inside, I saw the man pacing around his living room, seemingly talking to himself in between long swigs from his bottle. I could hear low mumblings, but I of course could not make out any words I understood.

When he had finished pacing, he collapsed into a brown leather recliner chair and became still. The nearly empty bottle slid from his fingertips and fell to the carpet, tumbling onto its side.

If I needed a car, this seemed to be the opportunity presenting itself.

I stepped down from the bucket and crept back through the narrow alley and up the street to the front of the house, leaving it behind.

First, I checked the Beetle. I twisted the handle to find it locked. I then ran my hand under the muddy wheel wells in hopes of a stashed key.

No luck.

I checked both bumpers before searching for a gas cap but could not find one.

"Dammit," I hissed under my breath before turning to the front door of the home the man had stumbled into.

"OK," I mumbled to myself. "Let's go get that key."

I crept up to the door and placed my hand on the handle before pausing for a brief moment to collect myself. I wasn't necessarily nervous about what might happen, I was mostly anticipating it being over.

I twisted the knob and the door gave. I pulled it open and peered inside. There, on the recliner lay the drunken man, asleep. The room was very plain in appearance. There were no pictures on the mantle above the fireplace and the walls were painted a dull green. A side table sat beside the recliner, littered with empty beer cans and an ashtray overflowed with cigarette butts onto the carpet, which looked marked with burn holes. I entered timidly.

My steps were light and cautious. I did not close the door behind me, choosing to leave it open a sliver in case a quick retreat was needed. I crossed the room and checked the side table with the beer cans for the keys but found nothing. I turned my head back toward the door to see if they had been hung up anywhere but that also proved fruitless. Now I focused my attention on the man in the chair. He was wearing nothing but a T-shirt and jeans. His jacket had seemingly been torn off upon his entry and lay sprawled on the carpet. He was a slightly large man who wore a size of jeans that were too small for his weight, causing the contents of his pockets to be outlined prominently in bulging shapes under the denim. It was then I found what I was looking for, but in order to get it, I'd have to inch my fingers into the front left pocket of his pants.

I began to do so tenderly and the drunken man stirred. Instinctively, I sprang away, but I continued to observe him until he had settled again. After a brief and breathless moment, I made another attempt.

With my fingers inside his front pocket I could feel the ring of his keys. I hooked my middle finger around it and began to pull. The man flinched again in his alcohol-induced sleep but went still before long. I continued pulling until I had the keys in my hand. But just as I went to turn and leave, his eyes shot open and he let out a haunting shriek, attempted to scamper away from me, and tumbled out of his chair backward onto the floor.

"*Geist! Geist!*" he bellowed, his face stricken with terror, his arms outstretched.

I don't know why—perhaps knowing I had no other way to defend myself if it came to that—but I found myself trying to reason with this man.

"No, no *geist!* No *geist!*" I knew not what *geist* meant, but it seemed apparent that I needed to convince this man I was not whatever that word meant. "No *geist!*"

I took a step toward him and he recoiled like a hand from a hot stovetop. He began babbling German words through hefty sobs.

"Relax," I said. "I'm not going to hurt you, I just need the car."

More words I didn't understand came tumbling from his mouth. I decided then that my attempts to calm him were futile.

"I'm going. I'm sorry," I said, feeling some kind of guilt for throwing this man into such a fumbling terror.

I back stepped across the room and searched for the door with my able hand splayed behind my back, not taking my eyes off the man. As I pushed the door open behind me, the man's expression seemed to change as if the fright had drained from his face with the suddenness of pulling a plug. I had never seen more sober eyes.

"I . . . buried . . . you," he mumbled, his face now completely blank and featureless.

I considered this but could not comprehend his meaning. Without further hesitation, I left his home.

I closed the door behind me and stormed the Beetle across the street. I observed the keys in my open palm and found the one with the Volkswagen logo on it and slid it into the lock. With a click, I heard the locks open and I cranked the handle. As I swung the door open, I heard a shot ring out from inside the house.

I looked back, however briefly, then returned my focus to the vehicle.

I eased myself into the Beetle and it accepted me with a gentle dip. I put the key in the ignition and glanced down at the gear shift.

Driving a manual vehicle was not an issue for me. *Operating* a manual vehicle with a crippled arm may prove problematic. Luckily for me, unlike cars in the States, the steering wheel was on the right hand side.

I figured I could operate the wheel and stick shift with my left hand, and with this hope, I turned the key and put the vehicle in gear.

Twenty-Two

I cannot describe the levels of exhilaration that rushed over my body like hot flame. I hollered and yelled and screamed and cried until I was light-headed.

As I roared down the road, I felt heat seeping from the vents in the dashboard. Carefully steadying the wheel with the top of my knee, I reached over and fully opened the vent, which blew warm air up my forearm. I felt my pores expand and drink in the heat as if I were a cold-blooded creature, thawing out my frozen center.

The rain drummed on the roof of the car and was cast off the windshield by fast-moving wiper blades. I was sheltered, warm, and careening toward my destination. I felt good.

I pulled off to the side of the road to address the map. I delicately removed it from the waistband of my striped trousers and peeled it open. It was wet and fragile so I handled it with the greatest of care.

Once I unfolded the map, I could see that some of the markings August had drawn had bled from the rain but they were still clearly intelligible. Luckily, the crucial information—the locations of the labor camps—was printed onto the map rather than drawn in ink.

I lay the map flat on the seat beside me, hoping the heat from the vents would dry it out by the time I got to where I needed to be. August had said it would take half a day to reach Asten by car, and it was beginning to get dark. I did not plan on stopping until I had gotten to my destination.

Slotting the gear shift into first, I rolled back onto the road and began my final push.

The setting sun cast a pinkish glow across the green German countryside as it sailed past my window. It was lovely and would have served as a gorgeous backdrop for a road trip given different circumstances. I drove on into the night.

I passed through Eisenach and down to Bad Hersfeld before going north around the completely decimated city of Kassel. I followed the 44 until transferring to the 3 just past Essen. I would soon be approaching the border between Germany and the Netherlands. The way my route had been planned, I was to punch through the border between two clusters of heavy fighting along the advancing American line into Germany. Soon I would have to leave the comfort of my precious Volkswagen and finish my journey on foot. Plowing a vehicle through an active combat zone surely meant death.

To think there would be an open gap in the line inviting me across was beyond naive. There would undoubtedly be some conflict I would have to cut through and that was terrifying. I could have made it all this way, overcoming everything that I had to be taken out by a stray bullet, or even worse, shot dead by one of my own men. That was something I couldn't concern myself with now.

The sounds of battle began to contest with the sound of the Volkswagens engine as I drove closer to the border. The roads were slick with rain but void of life. I debated stopping and beginning my final push on foot but decided to get a little closer by vehicle. This was the first of a series of crucial errors in judgment.

My second crucial error was choosing to leave the main road that had taken me this far to drive on more secluded side roads. Even calling them roads was generous. They consisted of mud and gravel, which would ultimately play a role in my impending disaster.

The final error came down to simple overconfidence.

With the finish line at the tips of my fingers, I fell into a narrow-focused fever. I developed tunnel vision and ignored all sensory information that may have aided me in avoiding catastrophe.

The roads bent and swerved like a meandering river, causing sharp, blind corners. They were difficult to maneuver with only one hand on the wheel, not to mention it not being my prominent one, but I had thought I could manage.

I knew I was going too fast. *I knew it!* But with the taste of the end so close to my tongue I disregarded these internal warnings.

The bomb was now set. The safety measures had all been ignored and it was only a matter of time before it went off.

As the approaching curve presented itself in front of me, I bounded toward it like all the ones that had come before. I failed to complete the turn, the wheel slipping from my clammy hand, and was launched from the mucky road. I bounced violently within the vehicle as I careened over the uneven countryside. Up ahead there was a tree approaching. There was no indication of slowing.

Twenty-Three

The impact was hard and sobering. My body was thrown into the steering wheel with such impenetrable force that the steering column snapped and the wheel was thrown about the interior of the vehicle. The air in my lungs was squeezed from my body as pain pierced my chest as if I had been scattered with fast-moving shrapnel.

The head-on collision crushed the front end of the Beetle like an aluminum can, forcing the dashboard into my thighs just above the knees, crushing my legs and pinning me to the seat.

I produced a sound I had never heard myself make and braced my arms against the buckled dashboard in a futile attempt to pull myself free. I moaned and growled in the newfound stillness but I was indeed trapped within the vehicle. I was sure that my legs were broken. That many of my ribs were broken. The fingers on my left hand bent and curled in unnatural ways and hot liquid ran down my face.

I struggled further with the crumpled dashboard that pressed my legs against the seat before my adrenaline dissipated completely and I slumped back in my seat, panting. I could only manage short and shallow breaths, as the pain in my chest was too great, and I lay in the morning sun as it passed through the broken glass of the windshield.

I ran my tongue throughout my mouth and found jagged points where my front teeth used to reside.

My head rolled to the left limply and my eyes fell on the map on the seat beside me, its dampness had kept it fixed to the leather like glue. I reached for it with crooked fingers and peeled it from the seat and brought it up to my chest, holding it snug like a newborn baby. Hopefully, whoever found me would see it in my arms and gather that I considered it precious. That whatever had been printed on its frail paper was of proper importance—as the contents of a dead man's hands often were—and retrieve it curiously. With this thought in mind, I let myself slip from the conscious world and retreated into the veil of nothingness.

A deep and painful breath awoke me in near total darkness. Reality came splashing over me like an obsidian wave on the shore of consciousness and I attempted to move, only to find new and deepening pains throughout my body.

Beyond the trees the blackened sky was broken up with flashes of artillery fire that cracked like thunder in delayed *pops* and *booms*. The fighting was drawing nearer. That meant we were *winning*. Maybe they would come to *me* and my journey would be over. But I had always been an impatient man.

I began another feeble attempt at prying my legs from the dashboard with no success. I no longer had any feeling in my legs as the blood flow had been interrupted, and this produced a dull panic that covered me like a blanket.

I managed to locate the steering wheel that had broken away from the steering column but struggled to pick it up from the floor or the passenger's side due to my mangled fingers. I brought my hand up to my face and observed my fingers in their sorry state. If I was to use my hand with any sort of efficiency, I had to set the bones right.

Bringing my hand across my body, I placed it in the other and grasped my fingers weakly. My right hand still did not have the strength to do what I needed it to, so instead I thrust my left arm forward into my palm and my fingers corrected with a palpable crunch.

I couldn't help but let out a sharp yelp, but pulling my hand away I discovered I had some maneuverability. Hopefully enough to grasp the steering wheel, my hope being I could use the broken steering column to pry the metal of the dashboard away from my legs and free myself.

I leaned to my left and tried to retrieve the wheel but I still could not get my fingers around it. Instead I fed my hand through the steering wheel and hooked my wrist around the inside and pulled it up that way. With some more finagling I thrust the steering column between the dashboard and the seat and began trying to create a gap for which I could free my legs from. Like everything else I had tried thus far, it was of no use.

This is when I began to become extremely frustrated. I slammed my hand against the dashboard despite the pain it produced and began shouting a slew of profanities. I was angry with everything, but mostly at myself.

Why had I chosen to drive so carelessly?

I shook my head bitterly and began pondering the *what-ifs.*

What if I'd stayed on the main road?

What if I hadn't brought Dieter to Hammes' cellar?

What if I'd stayed in my fox hole in the Ardennes Woods and never run from the war?

What.

If.

After my juvenile fit of self-pity and aimless anger had expired, I sat with my head hung low over my chest. The rain was still coming down and I leaned out of the window and held my open mouth under the sheet of water that ran from the top of the window frame. My mouth would fill with cold rain water, then I would swallow before repeating the process.

Once satisfied, I rested my head against the seat and a song crept into my mind.

"Oh, Danny boy, the pipes, the pipes are calling.
From glen to glen, and down the mountain side.
The summer's gone, and all the roses falling.
It's you, it's you must go and I must bide."

We Will Not Die Here

I went from a whisper to a low mumble.

"But come ye back when summer's in the meadow.
Or when the valley's hushed and white with snow.
I'll be here in sunshine or in shadow.
Oh, Danny boy, oh, Danny boy, I love you so."

My voice began to gain strength.

"But if ye come, when all the flowers are dying.
And I am dead, as dead I well may be.
You'll come and find the place where I am lying.
And kneel and say an Ave there for me."

Now I sang loud and unabashedly at the top of my voice.

"And I shall hear, tho' soft you tread above me.
And all my grave will warmer, sweeter be.
For you will bend and tell me that you love me.
And I shall sleep in peace until you come to me."

Twenty-Four

Rummaging throughout the glove box proved fruitless save for a lonesome pencil. I retrieved it and placed it in my right hand, which sat limp by my side on the seat. I took the map that was still faintly damp and flipped it over so it was facedown on the passenger's seat.

Grabbing my right arm by the wrist, I transferred it across my body and lay it on top of the map. The twisting of my torso ground my broken ribs against one another and took the air out of my lungs. The pain was petrifying. Despite this, I managed to position myself so I would be able to write what I needed to.

"My name is Henry Gerald Briggs. My father is Michael Briggs and my mother is Katherine Mary Briggs. They live on 114 Wascana Lane, New Hope, Pennsylvania. I would appreciate it greatly if whoever finds this could relay the following message to them:

I know I promised I would come back home to you but things just didn't play out that way. My mind was strong until the end but my body has all but given up on me. The things I have done, and the things I have endured are too grim to describe, but know I found peace within myself at the end. I love you both immensely, and I had all of you in my heart in my final moments.

Please do not dwell on my passing too harshly. This is war and death is as common here as flowers in spring or rain in September. Most men never get the chance to write a letter like this.

I must cut this short or I will write until I run out of room on this piece of paper. I love you all. I did all I could. I only wish I could have done more.

-Henry"

I let the pencil fall from my fingers, folded the map and placed it in my lap. The beast of war continued to roar ahead. All I could do now was wait for the American tide to wash over me. Whether I would be alive by the time that happened was uncertain.

I spent four days in that car. Escape was no longer the priority. Despite all my attempts to free myself there was no hope in doing so. I was trapped in every sense of the word.

When it rained, I drank. When I had to urinate, I went where I sat. But above all I kept the map safe. I had gotten it this far and the way the fighting was going it was only a matter of time before the Americans would reach me. I just tried to keep myself conscious for when that time arrived.

A putrid smell had begun to fill the inside of the vehicle. It was a smell I was all too familiar with in war: decomposition. My legs had begun to rot.

In a way I was thankful I could not see them. I knew what the decaying of dead flesh looked like and I wasn't sure my mind could handle that sight. One could only take so much.

My body was sickly thin. There wasn't an ounce of fat on me for it to absorb and I could feel myself withering.

I experienced vivid hallucinations in my attempts to stay awake. There was a night where my mother sat beside me in the car. She told me it was OK to let go, that I had done what I had set out to do, and that she was proud of me. She would run her fingers through my hair the way she used to when I was a little boy. It was so *calming*. But I told her I wasn't ready yet. Once the Americans arrived, I would go. That was the promise I made.

It had gotten to a point where I didn't know what was real and what was an illusion of my dying mind. I would see horses gallop past the windows as if in slow motion with war medals and ribbons woven into their flowing manes. I saw my three sisters harvesting crops in the field surrounding me. And I saw Dieter walking by.

"Dieter," I mumbled through dry, cracked lips. "Wait for me."

He turned and smiled and approached the car. Bending down, he placed his elbows on the window frame of the car door.

"Is August with you?" I asked, the words rattling in my throat.

"He's already there, my friend."

"Good, good." My head lolled back against the seat in relief and I shut my eyes "Have you come to get me?" I asked.

"Yes. I'm going to get you out of there," he said, but his voice was not his own.

"No, not yet. I need to wait for the Americans."

"We *are* the Americans," I heard him say, and when I opened my eyes It was the face of an American soldier looking back at me. Taking this for fantasy, I mumbled, "and I'm *Hitler*."

"In that case, then, I better get you in front of my captain."

Captain. That word seemed to pull me back from the blurry edge.

"Yes," I said, clawing through the fog. "Captain. I need to get something to your captain."

"Relax, buddy, first we gotta get you out of there," said the soldier, attempting to open the car door.

"No!" I took the map from my lap and thrust it into his chest. He brought his hand up to retrieve it.

"This has the location of every labor camp in Germany and across Europe. They have hundreds of thousands of prisoners. Please take this to your superior officers. They're dying."

The soldier looked from the map in his dirty hands up to my face, wide eyed.

"How did you get this?" he asked in almost a whisper.

I ignored his question. "Just get it to someone."

With that, my quest had been completed. I let out a breath of indescribable triumph despite how much it had taken from me.

I could feel my body begin to shut down, knowing it had served its purpose. My arms went limp and my head rolled forward in my chest.

To my left, my mother sat quietly with her hands crossed in her lap with the most beautiful smile on her face.

"I did it, Mom," I mumbled to her. "I'm done."

What followed was a haze of fleeting moments. A group of soldiers used their entrenching shovels and wedged them between the seat and the dashboard. Then I was lying on the ground outside the Beetle. The branches of the trees above me quivered against the dimming sky. Lifting. Bobbing. The roar of an engine. Flowing wind. I distinctly remember fierce pain rushing into my legs as blood attempted to circulate within them. It felt good.

PART IV:

PHANTOMS

"We leave something of ourselves behind when we
leave a place, we stay there, even though we go away.
And there are things in us that we can find again
only by going back there."
-Pascal Mercier

Epilogue

Buchenwald was liberated on the eleventh of April, 1945, a month after my rescue. Twenty-one thousand inmates were found in the camp, as the Germans had fled in anticipation of the Allied forces. There is some discrepancy, but records show that Buchenwald harbored 280,000 inmates in its span of operation from 1937 to 1945, 56,545 of whom perished from malnutrition and disease, though the numbers are believed to be higher.

At Buchenwald's largest occupancy, nearly 90,000 inmates were held there, though that number, too, has been contested. Some estimate it to be closer to 120,000. The camp was only designed to hold 8,000.

Camps like these were responsible for the deaths of six million Jews from 1941 to 1945 in what we now know as The Holocaust in Hitler's attempt to systematically exterminate the European Jewish population. Only one-third of that population survived.

The atrocities of the Holocaust were so unfathomable that a new word was devised to describe what had happened. That word was *genocide*.

Germany surrendered on the seventh of May, 1945, and the war in Europe was over.

I hopped from field hospital to field hospital until finally being returned by boat to the States where, despite all efforts to save them, I lost both legs to amputation. Other injuries I sustained included several broken ribs and fingers. Fractures in both femurs. My right elbow was shattered and my bicep was torn on the same arm. I had a punctured lung, a broken nose and right collarbone, and I lost a few teeth. All in all, I did a real number on myself.

My recovery was long and hard fought. I spent nine months in a veterans' hospital in Portland, Oregon, which I found to be an illogical choice on behalf of the US Army, being that Portland couldn't be any farther from my home state of Pennsylvania without falling off into the Pacific.

I returned home by train in January of 1946, to the elation of my family, who hadn't been able to see me since my return to the States. There, my recovery continued. I was given prosthetics for my legs but never truly adjusted to them. I walked with a jagged gait that left me self-conscious and embarrassed about my appearance. I would have preferred a wheelchair instead, but the damage inflicted to my right arm made operating a wheelchair nearly impossible.

I can still *feel* my legs. I can experience the feeling of curling and flexing my toes, even though they are no longer there. Some nights they ache and throb when I'm lying in bed and it frightens me. My mind just can't seem to let go.

I celebrated Dieter's birthday in my own way that January in 1946, a personal tradition I continue to this day. Like me, he would be an old man now, most likely with a family of his own and the proud owner of his father's shop repairing shoes, preparing his children for their turn to carry on the family business.

I worked on the family farm until my parents passed away, and my sisters and I sold the land. My functions were limited and I was mainly in charge of paperwork—invoices and the like. I had to learn to write with my left hand, a task that took years to get right, but I managed. After we sold the farm, I lived on disability on my own in New Hope. My sisters offered to house me but I did not want to be a burden on them. They all got married and started families, and I rarely saw them.

It took me twenty-five years before I could speak about what happened over in Europe. I experience crippling nightmares and suffer debilitating anxiety whenever it snows or I see smoke rising out of chimneys. Even today I cannot look at a bar of soap without feeling sick to my stomach and breaking out into a cold sweat, or a Volkswagen Beetle, for that matter. But in 1970, at the age of fifty, I decided I wanted to return to Germany. I cannot accurately describe the compulsion I had to do so, but in April of that year, I flew back to Buchenwald to be there for the twenty-fifth anniversary of its liberation. The camp serves as a memorial now, the clock above the entrance forever stands still at 3:15; the exact time the Americans arrived. It was then I learned what the words above the gate meant that greeted every incoming inmate. *To each his own.* To each his own indeed.

There, I met with those who had survived the treacherous labor camp—some younger, some older—and we cried together and held each other as we relived memories of that time. One of those men would even go on to become the chief rabbi of Israel. He was only eight years old when he was liberated from Buchenwald.

Most men were there with their families with beautiful children I hoped would never have to experience what their parents had gone through.

I learned that Avenir died back in 1945 during the revolt from a man who was there in the quarry. He told me his death was quick, though this brought little comfort. I had always figured he had died that day but it still hurt to find out he had. At least he was with his family now, wherever it is we go when this life ends.

I left early that day, choosing not to gather with the survivors after the ceremony. I had one more stop I needed to make.

In preparation for this trip I had done my research. First, I had hoped to find Patty, Dieter's American sweetheart, but I was unsuccessful in my attempts. I also attempted to find Hammes, but with only first names from twenty-five years ago, it was simply an impossible task.

Disheartening as it was, I turned my attention to the real reason I wanted to return to Germany: *Von Strauss Shoeworks* in Munich.

When I arrived at the quaint little shoe shop, I found a boy behind the worn counter who was a spitting image of my late friend.

"*Hallo,*" he said, and I returned the greeting.

I could not take my eyes from the boy. In truth, he was a young man, perhaps a few years older than Dieter had been.

"*Englisch?*" I said to him and he responded with, "Yes, sir. How may I help you?" with only a slight accent.

"Are you the son of the owners of this shop?" I asked.

"Nephew," he replied, standing stout and proper. "Is this regarding an appointment?"

"No, I was simply hoping I could speak with them."

"It is only my aunt here. My uncle died two years ago. May I ask what it is regarding?"

"I was a friend of Dieter and August. I would like to see her, if I may."

The boy looked as if he had seen a ghost but remained professional.

"I will retrieve her. Please, wait here."

The boy turned and vanished through a door behind the counter.

After a few moments, an elegant-looking woman came swooping from the door, her greying hair tied behind her head. She wore a leather apron over top of a light yellow summer dress. Her eyes were brimming with tears.

"You knew my sons?" she questioned with some hesitation in her body language. Now I began to well up, too.

"I did," I replied. "I did."

Annemarie was her name, and she closed the shop for the remainder of the day and we sat and talked about her boys. I told her of everything Dieter and I had been through. I told her about how he ensured we stop every so often so I could dry and warm my feet, and how I would most likely not have made it without him. I spoke of her other son, August, and how he was responsible for the liberation of camps such as Buchenwald, and in turn, may have brought an end to the war as a whole.

It may have been the most beautiful few hours of my life. Never had I shared such pure emotion with someone. I didn't realize it at the time, but I believe we both found closure that afternoon. Our lives, which had been so immeasurably stunted by the events of the war, could finally resume with hearts finally at ease.

Annemarie kissed my cheek and offered for me to stay the night as it was getting dark, but I respectfully refused. She said I was welcome anytime and gave me her address on a slip of paper for me to write to her. I thanked her and once again apologized that I had failed to bring her boys home. She told me that that was not my responsibility and thanked me for bringing her their stories.

I left her standing in the doorway of her shop, and flew home the following day.

We wrote frequently until her passing in 1978.

I returned once again to Germany for her funeral where the young boy who had greeted me at the shoe shop now had a young family of his own. He even named his firstborn Henry. I was extremely flattered.

While I was there I managed to find the grave of Avenir Akinfeev in the cemetery I took part in destroying that had since been rebuilt four years prior. It was a small plaque that only held his name, worn from the elements. I took a white handkerchief from my breast pocket and wiped it clean of moss and dirt. It did not shine but it was filthy no more. I left a half ration of bread on his grave.

Soon after returning home, I met a lovely woman by the name of Marjorie Sue Stilton, who I would go on to marry. We adopted a boy named Jack and lived a respectable life in New Hope where I reconnected with my sisters and we had dinner at my house every Sunday.

I never thought I would be a father but I was good at it. I like to think it came naturally to me.

In my sixties, I was paid a visit from my friend across the Delaware; Scotty Emms. I was delighted to hear that he had survived. The last image I had of Scotty was him wrestling with a German guard to ensure my escape from Buchenwald. I always harbored guilt in my heart for leaving him the way I did but he understood why it was so important I did so and held no ill will, bless his soul.

Scotty had quite the tale of his own, of journeying across Germany in search of rescue, which he found in the kindness of a family that took him in until the war was over. It was a kindness I knew well.

Like me, Scotty had been searching for some kind of closure in his old age. That is why he tracked me down.

Scotty struggled with alcoholism after the war. It's funny how sometimes those with the brightest smiles have the darkest demons. He had been divorced twice and had five children, some who have kids of their own now.

Scotty quit the booze the day his first grandchild was born and never touched another drink until his passing in 1998.

At the age of ninety-one, I was diagnosed with stage four pancreatic cancer and was given a life expectancy of six months. My family convinced me to write of my time during the Second World War and these pages are a result of that.

I think I have said all I needed to say. I have an appointment this afternoon. Forgive the spelling mistakes.

-Henry Gerald Briggs

Afterword by
Jack Briggs

My dad, Henry, passed away peacefully on August 9, 2011, five days after his ninety-second birthday.

Growing up, he never spoke to me about what he went through during the war. He never spoke to *anyone* about it. But I knew the toll it took on him. My dad came back from the war half a man physically—but mentally, he was twice as strong as any person I've ever known.

I remember when I was a young boy, he took me to the museum on a sunny summer day, where he donated all the war medals he had received. When I asked him why he was giving them away, he simply turned to me and said, "I did not deserve them."

The only time I ever saw my dad mad was on September 11, 2001, when the Twin Towers of the World Trade Center were struck by planes, hijacked by terrorists from the Middle East. He thought another world war was imminent and feared I would be drafted. He was adamant I never step foot on a battlefield.

Following his death, I followed his path across Europe. I went to the *Bois Jacques,* known to the Americans as the Jacks Woods near Foy, where the fox holes still remain from what we know now as the Battle of the Bulge. I visited the Buchenwald Memorial where all of the "blocks" where the inmates were kept had been burnt to the ground. I saw the incinerators with my own eyes and felt the cold iron of their doors with trembling hands. It was a truly haunting experience. The feeling of loss was immeasurable.

From Buchenwald, I backpacked across Germany to Asten, Netherlands, in an attempt to follow in my dad's footsteps. I saw Erfurt and Gotha, which have since been rebuilt, beautiful fairytale cities from another time.

I hoped to find the spot of my dad's crash, though it was near impossible to accurately locate. Luckily, military maps of the daily advances during that time can all be found online, so I had a ballpark idea of where it had happened. But even still, I was never able to find the precise spot.

Von Strauss Shoeworks still operates to this day in Munich, Germany. Upon my visit, I met with a man named Lukas Von Strauss, the nephew of Annemarie Von Strauss, and he spoke to me about the time my dad visited her in 1970. He spoke about how after that day she seemed to have found peace within herself and how he named his own boy after my dad, and I had the chance to meet him, as well.

It pains me my dad never got to meet my own children. I have one girl and one boy. My oldest, Jaime, will be starting school soon.

Thanks to this story, they will get a chance to know their Grandpa in a way that I never did growing up. I will make sure they know of his bravery and his sacrifice. Their Grandpa was a hero, regardless if he refused to call himself one.

My dad made me promise not to read his story until after he had passed, a promise I kept. I hope he wouldn't be too upset with me for publishing his harrowing tale, for I feel not only does it highlight his unflinching character, but also adds details about the Second World War that I was never taught in school.

Though he struggled with the idea of God his whole life, I hope he now has his answers.

I love you, Dad, wherever you may be. You will never be forgotten.

CPSIA information can be obtained
at www.ICGtesting.com
Printed in the USA
BVHW071059110921
616366BV00006B/176